Praise for

"This indispensable guide to corporations' networks of integrated production clearly show... classes of China and South Korea have taken the initiative in sponsoring their country's integration into an overall process of capitalist globalization which has not only been US-led but also dependent on American mass consumption. Its exposure of the costs to the working classes in each country make this book essential reading for all those looking beyond the unfortunately very limited alternatives addressed here to neoliberal free trade in postwar Europe and contemporary Latin America."

—**LEO PANITCH**, editor, *Socialist Register*;
co-author (with Sam Gindin), *The Making of Global Capitalism*

"Building upon his excellent in-depth studies of capitalist development in South Korea, Japan and China, Martin Hart-Landsberg takes his analysis to the next level by explaining the profound significance of the restructuring of the international organization of production with the creation of cross-border production networks and global (surplus) value chains. By focusing upon how the drive for profits has led transnational corporations to divide production into multiple components in different locations, Hart-Landsberg convincingly demonstrates that a nation-state framework is a distorting lens through which to analyze capitalist globalization. He shows, too, that reliance upon national accounting data is not only a barrier to a correct analysis of the world of international capital—it also makes changing that world difficult because it supports the appearance that workers of other nations are the enemy rather than the transnational corporations that divide and weaken all workers. Hart-Landsberg's stress upon the sphere of production is essential because it gives him particular insight into economic theory, neoliberalism and state policies designed to remove all existing barriers to transnational capital and as well to consider potential alternatives such as those being explored in Latin America."

—**MICHAEL A. LEBOWITZ**, professor emeritus, Simon Fraser University;
author, *The Contradictions of "Real Socialism"*

"What exactly is 'globalization'? Why does it matter for working people and how does it relate to neoliberalism and capitalism? Why are Chinese workers not the rivals of American workers but their potential allies? Why do workers all over the world suffer from unemployment, declining real wages, disappearing benefits and many other hardships? How can capitalist globalization be resisted and how can development be reoriented towards the common good? These are the questions Martin Hart-Landsberg brilliantly discusses and convincingly answers."

—**MINQI LI**, University of Utah; author,
The Rise of China and the Demise of the Capitalist World Economy

Capitalist Globalization

Consequences, Resistance, and Alternatives

by MARTIN HART-LANDSBERG

MONTHLY REVIEW PRESS
New York

Library of Congress Cataloging-in-Publication Data available from
the publisher

—

978-1-58367-352-2 pbk
978-1-58367-353-9 cloth

Monthly Review Press
146 West 29th Street, Suite 6W
New York, New York 10001

www.monthlyreview.org

5 4 3 2 1

Contents

Acknowledgments

I am pleased to publish this book with Monthly Review Press. MR Press has long served as an important outlet for timely and insightful analyses of capitalist globalization and efforts to create alternatives to it. In particular I want to thank Michael Yates, editorial director of the Press, for his suggestions which helped sharpen my arguments, and Erin Clermont for her copyediting.

I also want to thank *Monthly Review* and *Critical Asian Studies* for giving me permission to include previously published articles in this book.

To sum up, what is free trade, what is free trade under the present condition of society? It is freedom of capital. When you have overthrown the few national barriers which still restrict the progress of capital, you will merely have given it complete freedom of action.

—KARL MARX, *On the Question of Free Trade*, Speech to the Democratic Association of Brussels, January 9, 1848

The question of Free Trade or Protection moves entirely within the bounds of the present system of capitalist production, and has, therefore, no direct interest for us socialists who want to do away with that system.

Indirectly, however, it interests us inasmuch as we must desire as the present system of production to develop and expand as freely and as quickly as possible: because along with it will develop also those economic phenomena which are its necessary consequences, and which must destroy the whole system: misery of the great mass of the people, in consequence of overproduction. This overproduction, engendering either periodical gluts and revulsions, accompanied by panic, or else a chronic stagnation of trade; division of society into a small class of large capitalists, and a large one of practically hereditary wage-slaves, proletarians, who, while their numbers increase constantly, are at the same time constantly being superseded by new labor-saving machinery; in short, society brought to a deadlock, out of which there is no escaping but by a complete remodeling of the economic structure which forms its basis.

—FREDERICK ENGELS, *On the Question of Free Trade,* Preface to the 1888 English edition

Introduction

Times are tough in the United States. Unemployment is high; those with jobs suffer real wage declines and ever greater demands to work harder and longer. Household debt is up and wealth is down. Homelessness is growing. Health care is becoming a luxury. In sum, people are hurting, scared, and increasingly angry. Unfortunately, tough times do not automatically produce a clear understanding of the causes of these problems and the appropriate responses to them.

I wrote this book for three reasons. First, I wanted to show how and why the capitalist drive for profit has shaped a globalization process that is largely responsible for both our current problems and the dire future we face if state policies and corporate patterns of economic activity continue unchanged.

Of course, people talk about globalization all the time, and even economists admit that it has its costs. Still, the phenomenon is generally presented as both irreversible and overwhelmingly beneficial. In fact, most economists believe that the best way to respond to the costs of globalization is to embrace the process and improve our ability to compete more effectively against our national rivals. This requires, above all, greater freedom for market forces, which translates into further liberalization, deregulation, and privatization of economic activity. In other words, we have no one to blame but ourselves if we suffer from globalization.

This notion of globalization as a natural web of expanding ties between nations in which the invisible hand of competition can enhance efficiency and majority well-being holds powerful sway over people's thinking. It underpins the belief of many U.S. workers that our economic problems are primarily due to the policies of other governments, like that of China, who do not play fair: they restrict market forces and thus gain for their own citizens an undeserved advantage over U.S. corporations and workers. This belief, in turn, encourages working people to demand that the U.S. government compel these other governments to make their respective national economies operate more like our own. In short, this notion promotes the view that there is nothing fundamentally wrong with capitalism—we just need to defend it against problematic state interventions.

In contrast, as I argue in Part 1 of this book, "Capitalist Globalization," transnational corporations have shaped a global system of production and consumption that has created tremendously harmful international and national imbalances, instabilities, and inequities. In large measure this system has worked to boost transnational corporate profits by pitting workers from different countries against one another. A case in point: Chinese workers are not gaining at the expense of U.S. workers. Chinese workers are actually suffering from many of the very same problems as U.S. workers, including high unemployment, intensification of work processes, declining real wages and employment opportunities, and disappearing social benefits. They are not our rivals but potentially our allies in pursuing an alternative to existing patterns of production and consumption.

The many imbalances and instabilities created by capitalist globalization were for a time papered over by stock and housing bubbles in the United States and elsewhere. That time has now passed. As a result, transnational corporations have left us facing a likely future of stagnation, with growing numbers of people destined to experience worsening living conditions unless capitalist accumulation dynamics are confronted and transformed.

This brings me to the second reason I wrote this book: to expose the dominant theoretical approach used to demonstrate the superiority of market forces as an organizer of economic activity, neoliberalism, for being both a flawed theory and an ideological cover for the destructive transnational corporate political project highlighted above. Regardless of how bad conditions are, most people are reluctant to hold capitalism responsible. They end up supporting policies, such as free trade agreements, that actually enhance corporate mobility and power at their own expense. In large part this is because of the continuing ideological power of neoliberalism. Any call to restrict or replace corporate control over economic activity is met with derision by leading economists, as well as business and government leaders who point to this theory, and in particular the theory of comparative advantage, as proof that it is impossible to improve on market outcomes. Few people have the confidence to stand their ground in the face of this response.

Therefore, in Part 2 of this book, "The Neoliberal Project and Resistance," I critically examine the assumptions underlying the theory of comparative advantage and the numerous studies done by the World Bank, U.S. government, and mainstream economists that claim to prove the benefits of unrestricted international trade and investment. I do so to establish that this theory and these studies function much more as ideology than as social science. I also critically examine institutions like the World Trade Organization and agreements like the U.S.-Korea Free Trade Agreement to demonstrate that they wrap themselves in neoliberal justifications only to mask their main aim, which is to advance transnational corporate power regardless of social cost.

It is not enough to win theoretical arguments, even though it is important to give opponents of capitalism confidence in debates and when organizing. Thus I also evaluate the efforts of contemporary social movements to build popular resistance to institutions like the WTO and agreements like the U.S.-Korea Free Trade Agreement. Unfortunately, all too often these movements have pursued strategies that are counterproductive to their long-term goals. To combat this, I suggest criteria for movement building that I believe can help shape and encourage more effective organizing.

Finally, my third reason for writing this book is to encourage serious thinking about the institutions, policies, and practices needed to create an alternative to capitalist globalization. In "Alternatives to Capitalist Globalization," Part 3, I examine efforts by countries in South America and the Caribbean to advance a process of cooperative development. The most promising initiatives are under way in this region and I focus on the two most important: the Bolivarian Alliance for the Americas (ALBA) and the Bank of the South. I draw lessons from these and other attempts at cooperative development to suggest fruitful strategies for shaping a development process that emphasizes public rather than private ownership, domestic rather than export orientation, social rather than profit motivation, and solidaristic rather than competitive national relations. Although the outcome of current efforts remains unclear, I believe that our shared history of struggle and experimentation gives us good reason to be optimistic about the future.

PART I

CAPITALIST GLOBALIZATION

1—The Internationalization of Production and Its Consequences

We live in a time marked by growing international and national imbalances, instabilities, and inequities. What is not well understood is the connection between these threats to our well-being and contemporary capitalist dynamics.

Capitalism is not a static system. The levers driving its motion are capital accumulation, competition, and class struggle. Their complex interplay generates pressures and contradictions that compel profit-seeking capitalists to continually reorganize their activities, a process that has profound consequences for our lives. In other words, our social condition is largely shaped by the actions of the leading business organizations.

Today, these business organizations are transnational corporations. As we shall see, their drive for profit has produced a new, more globalized stage of world capitalism, one shaped by dynamics that are directly responsible for generating the imbalances, instabilities, and inequities that threaten our well-being. Most important, this means that the economic and social challenges we face have deep structural underpinnings. As a consequence, efforts at reform that accept the logic of existing patterns of economic activity will prove unable to satisfy our pressing need for meaningful social change.

The Growth and Transformation of International Production

Transnational corporations (TNCs) are more than just large companies with a global reach. They now direct a significant share of global economic activity. According to the *World Investment Report 2011*, "TNCs worldwide, in their operations both at home and abroad, generated value added of approximately $16 trillion in 2010, accounting for more than a quarter of global GDP. In 2010, foreign affiliates accounted for more than one-tenth of global GDP and one-third of world exports."[1]

Transnational corporations tend to be among the largest and most powerful firms in their respective home countries. At the same time, as Table 1.1 shows, international operations now account for the majority of the assets, sales, and employment of the 100 largest non-financial TNCs. Looking at all TNCs, the value added by their foreign affiliates rose from approximately 35 percent of total value added in 2005 to 40 percent in 2010.[2]

The current centrality and internationalization of transnational corporate production is the result of a long and competitive process.[3] In broad-brush, foreign direct investment (FDI) in the first decades after the Second World War was primarily motivated by the desire of transnational corporations to gain access to foreign markets protected by high tariffs. U.S. TNCs were the primary international investors during this period. Although important, these newly established foreign operations were generally viewed by their parent companies as supplementary to their home country investments.[4]

The motivation for, and nature of, foreign direct investment began to change in the late 1960s. In response to a growing

TABLE 1.1: Internationalization Statistics of the 100 Largest Non-Financial TNCs (bns of dollars, thousands of employees, and pcnt.)

Variable	2008	2009	2010
Assets			
Foreign	6,161	7,147	7,512
Total	10,790	11,543	12,075
Foreign as % of total	57	62	62
Sales			
Foreign	5,168	4,602	5,005
Total	8,406	6,979	7,847
Foreign as % of total	61	66	64
Employment			
Foreign	9,008	8,568	8,726
Total	15,729	15,144	15,489
Foreign as % of total	57	57	56

Source: UNCTAD, *World Investment Report 2011* (New York: UN, 2011), 27.

decline in profit margins caused by the combination of increasingly successful Japanese and European export activity aimed at the U.S. market and rising domestic wages, U.S. transnational corporations began establishing "export platforms" in select third world countries. Parts and components were sent to these export platforms; low-wage third world workers performed operations on them; and the intermediate products were shipped back to the United States for final assembly and sale. Although these foreign operations were limited to relatively simple labor-intensive tasks, their activities were integral to home-country operations and profitability.

The mid-1980s marked the start of the third and current stage in the internationalization of production, one marked by a sharp acceleration in foreign direct investment. Foreign direct investment grew far more rapidly in the 1980s than world trade and world output, "increasingly becoming an engine of growth in the world economy."[5] Between 1983 and 1989, world foreign direct investment outflows grew at a compound annual growth rate of 28.9 percent, compared with a compound annual growth rate of 9.4 percent for world exports and 7.8 percent for world gross domestic product.[6]

Again, this development was primarily the result of intensified competition between U.S. corporations and those from Japan and Germany. More Japanese and German exports to the United States gave these foreign corporations an ever larger share of the U.S. market, especially in higher-value-added manufactures, producing, among other things, a rapidly increasing U.S. trade deficit. Negotiations between the U.S., Japanese, and German governments aimed at reducing this deficit culminated in the 1985 Plaza Accord, which called for a significant increase in the value of Japanese and German currencies relative to the dollar. This outcome stimulated companies from both countries, especially Japan, to shift selected core operations to countries with more favorable currency rates and labor costs. East Asia was an especially attractive location for Japanese TNCs.[7]

Thus, while U.S. corporations had been the primary drivers of the internationalization of production until the mid-1980s, after that period TNCs from other countries began aggressively pursuing their own international strategies.[8] In fact, outflows of foreign direct investment from Japan exceeded those from the United States beginning in 1986. In 1989 Japan became the largest source country of foreign direct investment flows, accounting for 23 percent of the total FDI outflows that year.[9]

This new stage was also marked by a change in TNC accumulation dynamics. Previously, transnational corporations had used export platforms to cheapen the production cost of labor-intensive and technologically simple goods such as garments and basic consumer electronics. The transnational corporate investment that began in the mid-1980s was undertaken to produce far more sophisticated manufactures. By the 1990s, these goods included automobiles, televisions, computers, power and machine tools, cameras, cell phones, pharmaceuticals, and semiconductors.

More important, the change in product line was coupled with a major restructuring in the organization of production. In brief, TNCs began dividing their production processes into ever finer segments, both vertical and horizontal, and locating the separate stages in two or more countries, creating what are commonly called cross-border production networks or global value chains. The Asian Development Bank offered the following description of the change:

> In its formative years in the early 1990s, production sharing involved moving small fragments of the manufacturing process to low-cost countries and importing their component outputs to the host country for the last-stage fabrication.
>
> Later, production networks became more intricate, with firms in different countries having charge of different stages of production, thus resulting in product fragments crossing multiple borders prior to final product assembly in the host country. More recently, with international supply networks of parts and components now well established, firms have also started setting up final-assembly processes for a broad range of consumer durables (such as computers, cameras, televisions, and automobiles) abroad, both to take advantage of cheap labor and to be closer and more responsive to niche markets.
>
> Today, cross-border trade in parts and components has developed into a truly global phenomenon, although it plays a far more important role for developing Asia than for other developing regions, given the region's integration with the world economy. Particularly with the emergence of the PRC [People's Republic of China] as the premier final-assembly center of electronics and related products since the mid-1990s, intraregional flows of both parts and components and final goods have recorded phenomenal growth.[10]

The adoption of this new transnational corporate strategy greatly increased the importance of the third world as a location for international production. As a consequence, the third world share of world foreign direct investment began a slow and steady rise in the late 1980s. The current centrality of the third world to transnational production is highlighted by the fact that in 2010, for the first time, more than half of all FDI went to third world and transition economies.[11] As Tables 1.2a and 1.2b show, this outcome is the result of developed as well as developing and transition country TNCs shifting their investment activity to the third world.

Although core country TNC dominance of cross-border production networks remains strong, international competitiveness pressures have led to a constant process of change in their organizational structure. In particular, many core country TNCs have come to rely on independent "partner" manufacturers to procure required parts and components and oversee their assembly into final products. Some, but not all, of these partner manufacturers are themselves transnational in their operation. In many cases, these partner TNCs are headquartered in the third world. One consequence of this development: a growing number of core country transnational corporations are no longer directly involved in production. Rather they maintain control over their production networks through their control over product design and marketing.

The most common non-equity modes (NEM) of transnational corporate control and coordination are contract manufacturing, services outsourcing, contract farming, franchising, licensing, and management contracts. Firms operating under NEM arrangements employed approximately 20 million workers and generated over $2 trillion in sales in 2010, with contract manufacturing and services outsourcing by far the most important.[12]

Although the use of NEM-organized production varies considerably across industries, it is especially important in those with significant labor-intensive operations. For example, contract manufacturing activity accounts for an estimated 90 percent of

TABLE 1.2a: Distribution of FDI Projects by Developed Country TNCs

Receiving Region	2007	2010
Developed Economies	68%	51%
Developing Economies	26%	45%
Transition Economies	6%	4%

Source: UNCTAD, *World Investment Report 2011* (New York: UN, 2011), 8.

TABLE 1.2b: Distribution of FDI Projects by Developing and Transition Country TNCs

Receiving Region	2007	2010
Developed Economies	38%	30%
Developing Economies	58%	63%
Transition Economies	5%	7%

Source: UNCTAD, *World Investment Report 2011* (New York: UN, 2011), 8.

the production cost of toys and sporting goods, 80 percent of the production cost of consumer electronics, 60 to 70 percent of the production cost of automotive components, and 40 percent of the production cost of generic pharmaceuticals.[13] And, not surprisingly given the export emphasis of cross-border production, in 2010 contract manufacturers accounted for more than 50 percent of world exports of toys, footwear, garments, and electronics.[14] Moreover, there is every reason to believe that TNC reliance on NEM-structured activity will become even more important in the future; the growth of NEM sales over the years 2005 to 2010 outpaced the growth of overall industry sales in electronics, pharmaceuticals, footwear, retail, toys, and garments.[15]

The nature of NEM-participating firms varies by industry. As the *World Investment Report 2011* explained:

In technology and capital-intensive industries a small number of NEMs—often TNCs—dominate. In automotive components, pharmaceuticals and ITBPO [information technology and business process outsourcing] companies from developed countries are the largest contract manufacturers, while in electronics and semiconductors the situation is more mixed, but with developing country companies the more significant. In the case of labor-intensive industries such as garments, footwear and toys, however, a number of developing country TNCs act as intermediaries or agents between lead TNCs and NEMs, managing the manufacturing part of the GVC [global value chain].[16]

To the extent that participating firms are not themselves transnational, it means that TNC dominance over international economic activity is greater than previously stated. And to the extent that these firms are themselves transnational, it means that contemporary capitalist accumulation dynamics have given rise to a hierarchically structured, interlocking system of TNCs.

Case Study: The Electronics Industry

The electronics industry, which is one of the most reliant on this new form of international production, provides an excellent illustration of its workings. According to the *World Investment Report 2011*:

Contract manufacturing in the electronics industry evolved early. Offshoring up to the mid-1980s took the form of manufacturing FDI, as TNCs took advantage of cheaper, relatively skilled labor in host countries to process and assemble intermediate goods for shipping back to their home economies. In the latter part of the 1980s, a number of electronics companies started shedding manufacturing operations to concentrate on R&D, product design and brand management. The manufacturing was taken up by electronics manufacturing services (EMS) companies, including Celestica, Flextronics and

Foxconn. Some of these emerged from existing suppliers, especially those based in Taiwan Province of China (e.g. Foxconn); others were spinoffs, such as Celestica from IBM.

A small number of contract manufacturers now dominate the industry, with the largest 10 by sales accounting for some two-thirds of the EMS activity. They produce for all major brands in the industry, from Dell and Hewlett-Packard in computing to Apple, Sony and Philips in consumer electronics, with overall sales in electronics contract manufacturing amounting to $230–$240 billion in 2010.

All but three of the top 10 players in electronics contract manufacturing are headquartered in developing East Asia—the bulk of manufacturing production in the industry is centered in East and South-East Asia, particularly China. During the last decade, however, contract manufacturing firms in the industry have accelerated their spread to other regions, often by purchasing manufacturing facilities from lead TNCs.[17]

The production of Apple products, in particular the iPhone and iPad, highlights why core country transnational corporations embrace cross-border production. Apple introduced the iPhone in 2007. Sales in the United States soared from 3 million units in 2007 to over 11 million in 2009. Global sales topped 25 million in 2009. Apple designs the iPhone but contracts with nine different companies from four different countries (Japan, South Korea, Germany, and the United States) for the required components. These firms ship their products to China, where Foxconn (a Taiwanese-owned company) oversees their assembly and export to the United States and the rest of the world.

According to an Asian Development Bank study, the estimated 2009 production cost of Apple's 3G iPhone was $178.96 per phone. Although China was the host country for the final assembly, its value-added contribution was largely limited to its labor, which amounted to only $6.50 per phone; no domestic Chinese firms participated in the production network.[18] With a United States selling price of $500, the authors of the study estimated that Apple enjoyed a 64 percent profit margin on each phone sold in the United States.[19]

A follow-up study based on 2010 data for both the iPad and next-generation iPhone reinforces this picture of international production dynamics. Both products are produced by an Apple-organized cross-border production network. And not surprisingly, Apple enjoys the lion's share of the profits, approximately 30 percent of the sales price of its low-end iPad and 58 percent of the sales price of its 4G iPhone. Other participants enjoy far more modest rewards. For example, "The next biggest beneficiaries in the iPad and iPhone supply chains are Korean companies such as LG and Samsung, who provide the display and memory chips, and whose gross profits account for 5 percent and 7 percent, respectively, of the sales price for the iPhone and iPad. United States, Japanese and Taiwanese suppliers capture 1–2 percent each."[20]

Apple's production strategy highlights the inadequacies of using a nation-state framework to measure economic gains and losses. For example, China was credited with exporting 11.3 million iPhones to the United States in 2009. At a unit price of $179, this trade produced a U.S. trade deficit with China of slightly more than $2 billion. Subtracting the cost of components produced by U.S. corporations still leaves a U.S. trade deficit with China of approximately $1.9 billion. However, as we have seen, only $6.50 of each iPhone was generated by Chinese activity; the remaining value came from components produced by foreign corporations operating in other countries. Thus, in value terms, China's net trade gain was only $73.45 million. In short, although national accounting implies that China is the big winner and the United States the big loser, in reality the profit generated by the production and sale of iPhones was largely captured by a select few transnational corporations, none of which are Chinese, with Apple, a U.S. company, the biggest winner.[21]

Apple clearly maintains tight control over its production network, changing partner firms when it suits its purpose. It initially used Japanese suppliers to produce key components for its iPod.

It dropped them in favor of Korean firms, especially Samsung, for production of key components for its iPhone and iPad. Apple also replaced Silicon Valley chipmaker PortalPlayer, the supplier of a key microprocessor for an early version of these products, with Samsung.[22] Apple's production strategy also highlights the complex and contradictory nature of transnational corporate relations: Samsung is simultaneously participating in Apple's global value chain and developing and producing its own competing phones and tablets.

The Internationalization of Transnational Corporate Interests

The current stage of capitalist accumulation is one in which the interests of leading transnational corporations have become increasingly detached from their respective home economies. This situation is perhaps best summed up by the title of a *New York Times* article: "Invest Globally, Stagnate Locally."[23] As the author of the article noted, "In the United States and Europe, there has been a curious disconnect in recent years between the performance of the corporate sector and the performance of the overall economy."[24] A French analyst quoted in the article added: "All in all, the widespread prosperity of companies does not lead to prosperity for domestic economies or wage earners in Germany, France or Japan."[25]

This disconnect between corporate profitability and home-country economic conditions is encouraged by transnational capital's cross-border production strategy. The *New York Times* article explained why this is so:

> In Europe, where unions remain strong, the growing ability and desire of French and German companies to invest beyond borders gives management new leverage over labor. . . .
>
> The heightened mobility of capital allows companies to invest their profits around the globe with considerable

freedom. "American companies really haven't been sinking much of their gains back into domestic investment," said Jared Bernstein, senior economist at the Economic Policy Institute in Washington.

Thanks to globalization and the opening of new markets, Mr. King [chief economist at HSBC in London] said, "It's increasingly difficult to argue that companies themselves are attached to a country."[26]

As noted above, the leading firms in most core countries are significantly internationalized. The companies listed on the leading German stock index, the DAX 30, have only 53 percent of their employment and 34 percent of their sales in Germany. The percentages for firms listed on the French index, the CAC 40, are 43 percent and 35.5 percent respectively. Companies listed in the U.S. stock index the, S&P 500, appear to be more domestically centered, relying on the U.S. market for approximately 60 percent of their sales. However, the larger the company the more globalized its operation. In fact, the international share of U.S. corporate profits has been rising rapidly over the last three decades, from only 10 percent in the late 1970s to over 35 percent in 2007.[27]

International operations are valuable to U.S. transnational corporations not only because they are directly profitable but also because they offer these firms the ability to shelter their profits (regardless of where they are earned) in countries where tax rates are low. The size of accumulated overseas profits held by leading U.S. corporations as of 2010, as well as the overseas share of their 2010 pre-tax profits and 2010 revenue, is shown in Table 1.3. According to *BusinessWeek*, "For 30 big companies, the profits kept abroad grew 560 percent, to $740 billion, from the end of 2000 to the end of 2010."[28] For many firms, their overseas share of profits is considerably higher than their overseas share of revenue.

Though I have been focusing on transnational manufacturers and the ways in which their profit strategies have promoted the internationalization of production, transnational retailers are

TABLE 1.3: Overseas Profits of U.S. TNCs

Company	Accumulated Profits Held Abroad as of 2010 (bns.)	Overseas Share of 2010 Pre-Tax Profits	Overseas Share 2010 Revenue
GE	94.0	84%	53%
Pfizer	48.2	100%	57%
Merck	40.4	30%	56%
Johnson & Johnson	37.0	62%	52%
Exxon-Mobil	35.0	85%	74%
Citigroup	32.1	93%	59%
Cisco	31.6	88%	48%
IBM	31.1	54%	70%
P&G	30.0	44%	62%
Microsoft	29.5	62%	42%
Abott Labs	26.8	100%	57%
PepsiCo	26.6	51%	47%
Hewlett-Packard	21.9	63%	65%
Chevron	21.3	80%	58%
Coca-Cola	20.8	49%	70%
Eli Lilly	19.9	55%	45%
JPMorgan	19.3	34%	22%
Bank of America	17.9	100%	21%
Goldman Sachs	17.7	47%	45%
Google	17.5	54%	52%
Amgen	17.2	58%	23%

Source: Peter Coy and Jesse Drucker, "Profits on an Overseas Holiday," *Bloomberg Businessweek*, March 21, 2011.

also significant players in determining the structure and location of many production networks. They have also embraced the internationalization of production because it reduces the production costs of the goods they sell, thereby increasing their profits. Transnational financial service companies have also benefited from the expansion of cross-border production activity. Such activity not only generates concentrated profits in search of the highest return but also creates economic imbalances that need to be financed. These profits normally flow to leading core-country financial service companies, leaving them well placed to profit from the borrowing needs of governments and workers.[29] In short, there are no fundamental conflicts of interest among transnational corporations operating in different sectors regarding the benefits of the internationalization of production.[30]

A New International Architecture

The successful expansion of global accumulation has depended heavily on the creation of a new international architecture capable of providing the long-term economic certainty required by transnational capital. This architecture was largely built by state action, more specifically state-negotiated international trade/investment agreements and national regulatory changes. The fact that a diverse group of states continue to pursue policies that significantly limit their own authority over economic activity highlights the existence of a common class interest shared by transnational capital, one that transcends national and competitive differences.

The movement to create the new international architecture began during the late 1970s. The *World Investment Report 1991* described the process as follows:

> The trend toward reducing restrictions on the activities of transnational corporations in host developing countries is one of the more important policy developments of the past decade. A sample of more than 300 instances of changes in policies and regulations affecting foreign direct investment by transnational corporations covering 46 countries (20 developed market economy countries and 26 developing countries, including five newly industrializing countries) over 11 years (1977–1987) illustrates the scope and direction of the changes. More than two-thirds of the changes in the sample were in the direction of reducing restrictions on the activities of transnational

corporations. In the case of the newly industrializing countries, more than three-fourths of the changes were in the direction of reducing restrictions on transnational corporations.[31]

Perhaps the most important development in this movement was the successful push by the United States for a new, expanded round of the General Agreement on Tariffs and Trade (GATT). The resulting Uruguay Round began in 1986 and culminated in the establishment of the WTO in 1995. Although GATT traditionally was concerned only with tariff reductions on manufactured goods, this round took up a number of additional issues, including those related to foreign direct investment. The *World Investment Report 1991* provided this overview of the expanded agenda:

> One of the new issues being discussed in the Uruguay Round concerns trade-related investment measures (TRIMs), such as incentives and performance requirements for transnational corporations wishing to invest in a host country. Local content rules (that a given percent of a good must be domestic in order to be treated as "local" and, hence, be sold free of duty), trade balancing (that imports must be matched with a given amount of exports), and export-performance requirements are among the most familiar TRIMs, which can take on a variety of forms and degrees of applicability. The United States was instrumental in having TRIMs included in the current round of negotiations; it has been estimated that one-half of the latter's foreign direct investments in developing countries were subjected to TRIMs.[32]

Japan joined the United States in strongly opposing the right of governments to place requirements and restrictions on foreign direct investment and, with the support of European governments, they succeeded in securing a new agreement as part of the WTO—the Agreement on Trade-Related Investment Measures (TRIMs)—which made them illegal.[33] Other agreements with a similar aim were also approved and incorporated into the WTO.[34] These WTO agreements, as well as the many complementary multilateral and bilateral international investment agreements (IIAs) approved in the previous and following years, have created a critical supporting infrastructure for the expansion of transnational corporate activity, especially the successful operation of cross-border production networks. Generally, they ensure that transnational corporations will be able to

- import and export goods free from tariffs and non-tariff barriers.
- move funds across borders free from capital controls and other financial restrictions.
- invest without fear of performance requirements, which might require them to transfer technology, merge, or form alliances with local enterprises, hire local employees, or purchase local inputs.
- invest without fear that host governments might nationalize or restrict their operations in ways that reduce their profitability.

Developed capitalist country governments initially preferred using multilateral agreements to shape the new TNC-friendly international architecture. However, after enjoying some success, progress was halted by third world resistance as well as competitive differences between advanced capitalist countries. The WTO process collapsed in acrimony in 1999, and attempts to restart it have largely failed. As a consequence, most agreements are now bilateral. Free Trade Agreements (FTAs) are the most sweeping of these new bilateral agreements, including, among other things, provisions promoting foreign direct investment, capital mobility, and trade liberalization.

These agreements have become especially popular within East Asia, reflecting the region's critical role in transnational capital's cross-border production strategy. The members of ASEAN (Association of Southeast Asian Nations) were the first to embrace

FTAs, creating the ASEAN Free Trade Area (AFTA) in 1992. This agreement was designed to increase ASEAN's attractiveness to foreign investment by eliminating restrictions on the movement of goods (especially parts and components) from one country to another. In 1999, ASEAN countries joined with China, Japan, and Korea to establish the ASEAN Plus Three (APT) forum. The aim of this forum was to create a full-blown regional FTA, but that attempt failed, largely because of competitive differences between elites in China, Japan, and South Korea.

As transnational corporations began incorporating China more directly into their production networks, ASEAN and China were pressed to solidify their relationship. In 2002, they concluded a free trade agreement, the first in the region since AFTA. The Japanese government, fearful that this agreement might place Japanese firms at a competitive disadvantage, responded by signing an FTA with Singapore in 2002, a limited Comprehensive Economic Partnership Agreement with ASEAN in 2003, and then FTAs with Malaysia in 2006, Thailand and Indonesia in 2007, and ASEAN in 2008. South Korea, a late starter, completed an FTA with Singapore in 2005, and ASEAN in 2006. Korea and China began FTA discussions in 2010.

East Asian governments have also pursued and signed FTAs with countries outside the region. They did this for a number of reasons: many production networks include TNCs headquartered outside the region and a majority of the region's exports of final products are aimed at markets outside the region. In addition, the region's more developed countries host powerful transnational corporations whose operations are not limited to participation in East Asian–centered production networks or whose exports may compete with those produced by companies that do. Their governments need to ensure an attractive international investment and export environment for their leading corporations or risk losing them. For example, South Korea concluded FTAs with both the United States and Europe in 2011.[35]

All together, 119 FTAs were negotiated in the Asia-Pacific region between 2002 and 2006. During this period, China negotiated or proposed FTAs with 28 different countries. By comparison, the total was 21 for the European Union and 10 for the United States.[36]

While negotiations have been especially intense in the Asian region, governments throughout the world have pursued and signed a variety of international agreements designed to promote the internationalization of production. And, as the *World Investment Report 2011* makes clear, their efforts have not slackened:

> At the end of 2010 the IIA universe contained 6,092 agreements, including 2,807 bilateral investment treaties (BITs), 2,976 double-taxation treaties (DTTs) and 309 "other IIAs," [a category that includes FTAs and economic partnership agreements]. The trend seen in 2010 of rapid treaty expansion—with more than three treaties concluded every week—is expected to continue in 2011, the first five months of which saw the conclusion of 48 new IIAs (23 BITs, 20 DTTs and five "other IIAs") and more than 100 free trade agreements and other economic agreements with investment provisions currently under negotiation.[37]

The internationalization of production has also been encouraged by national policies, especially those designed to open new sectors or provide new benefits to encourage foreign investment. For example, in 2010, 74 countries adopted 149 policy measures affecting foreign investment. One hundred and one, or 68 percent, of those measures liberalized or promoted foreign direct investment.[38] Asian countries were among the most active, approving a "relatively high number of measures [to] ease entry and establish conditions for foreign investment."[39] In sum, the globalization of capitalist accumulation is best understood as a political project in which states have collectively and individually provided critical support for its expansion.

East Asia Restructured

To this point, I have discussed transnational corporate dynamics without rooting them at the nation-state level, a necessary step if we are to understand the specific ways in which these dynamics have produced our current imbalances, instabilities, and inequities. The obvious geographic starting point for concretizing the analysis is East Asia, which includes countries in both Northeast and Southeast Asia. As the Asian Development Bank noted, East Asia has become the center for transnational corporate cross-border activity. As a consequence, developing Asia's share of world GDP has steadily climbed, from less than 10 percent in 1980 to 28 percent in 2010.[40]

The expansion of cross-border production across East Asia has had a significant effect on the region's economic activity. Most obviously, it increased the region's trade dependency. East Asia's export-GDP ratio grew from approximately 15 percent in 1982 to 45 percent in 2006, far outstripping the growth in trade by both low- and middle-income developing countries and the world (see Table 1.4). As a result, developing Asia's share of world exports has grown considerably, from 8 percent in 1980 to nearly 26 percent in 2009.[41]

In line with TNC priorities, it has also led to an increase in the share of East Asian exports that are manufactures. For example, "Since the early 1990s, the share of manufactured exports to total exports in Southeast Asian countries (other than for Indonesia and the Philippines) has exceeded 70 percent. In the Philippines, the share of manufactured exports to total exports increased significantly after 1996, to more than 90 percent in 1996–2006 from 50 percent in 1991–1995."[42]

Within the broad category of manufactures, the emphasis has been on the export of machinery and transport equipment. As the Asian Development Bank explained:

TABLE 1.4: The Share of Exports in GDP (percent)

Year	World	Low- and Middle-Income Developing Countries	East and Southeast Asia
1982	16.35	14.70	16.64
1983	15.58	15.00	15.42
1984	15.97	15.81	16.00
1985	15.30	14.35	14.96
1986	14.18	12.02	15.56
1987	14.72	14.05	20.34
1988	15.09	14.39	21.13
1989	15.50	14.56	20.44
1990	15.95	15.51	21.77
1991	15.55	15.71	22.52
1992	15.58	16.50	23.36
1993	15.17	16.69	23.67
1994	15.99	17.99	24.66
1995	17.47	19.57	24.89
1996	17.92	19.88	24.49
1997	18.67	20.31	26.92
1998	18.50	20.32	29.62
1999	18.43	22.23	28.33
2000	20.11	25.00	31.86
2001	19.40	24.32	30.15
2002	19.49	25.80	31.57
2003	20.22	27.64	35.67
2004	21.82	30.02	40.28
2005	22.94	31.22	42.94

Source: Asian Development Bank, *Asian Development Outlook 2007* (Philippines: Asian Development Bank, 2007), 57.

The share of these exports in the region's total manufacturing exports rose from about 36 percent in 1992 to 55 percent in 2006. Machinery and transport equipment exports have increased significantly in East and Southeast Asia, accounting for more than half of manufactured exports in 2006. For the Philippines and Malaysia, the share of this component in manufactured exports was about 80 percent in 2006, while it was around 70 percent in Korea and Singapore.[43]

And, within this sector, the emphasis has been on the export of information and communication technology (ICT) products (such as computers and office machines; and telecom, audio, and video equipment) and electrical goods (such as semiconductors). Developing Asia's share of world exports of ICT products increased from 25 percent in 1992 to 50 percent in 2006. Developing Asia's share of world exports of electrical goods also soared, from 16 percent in 1992 to 36 percent in 2006.[44] These two product lines together accounted for almost three-fourths of total exports from East Asia in 2006-7.[45]

The central role of cross-border production networks in knitting together East Asia's economic activity is perhaps best highlighted by the growing importance of parts and components in the region's trade. As Table 1.5 shows, the share of parts and components in developing Asia's total manufacturing exports rose from 17.3 percent in 1992-93 to 34 percent in 2006-7. The share of parts and components in developing Asia's total imports of manufactures rose from 29 percent to 44.2 percent over the same period. Even more telling is that parts and components now make up more than half of all intraregional exports and imports. By comparison the figure is only 36.3 percent for NAFTA countries and 22.1 percent for EU15 intraregional trade.[46]

Moreover, the region's trade in parts and components is dominated by ICT products and electrical goods. For example, "Semiconductors and other electronics components alone accounted for 50 percent of component exports from East Asia in 2006-7. Adding components of telecommunication equipment and office and automated data-processing machines to these items increases the concentration ratio to almost 90 percent of total exports of components."[47] In short, East Asian export production (itself a growing share of total national production) has increasingly narrowed, not only to parts and components but to a select few in response to the needs of transnational corporate-controlled production networks.

China, as previously noted, plays a key role in transnational capital's regional production strategy. In the words of the Asian Development Bank, "The increasing importance of intraregional trade is attributed mainly to the parts and components trade, with the PRC functioning as an assembly hub for final products in Asian production networks."[48] The share of parts and components in China's imports of manufactures from East Asia rose from less than 24 percent in 1992–93 to over 59 percent in 2006–7. The import share of parts and components in the machinery and transportation equipment category climbed from 46.1 percent in 1994–95 to 73.3 percent in 2006–7.[49] It is China's unique position as the region's production platform that enabled the country to increase its share of world exports of ICT products from 3 percent in 1992 to 24 percent in 2006, and its share of electrical goods from 4 percent to 21 percent over the same period.[50]

As a result of transnational capital's restructuring of East Asian economic activity, East Asia's exports (with the major exception of China) have shifted from the United States and the European Union to East Asia, and in particular China. China, in contrast, has shifted its export emphasis away from East Asia toward the United States and the European Union. Between 1992–93 and 2004–5, the East Asian share of China's final goods exports declined from 49.5 percent to 26.5 percent, whereas the OECD share (excluding Japan and South Korea) increased from 29.3 percent to 50.1 percent.[51]

With East Asia now focused on exporting parts and components in support of China-based export production, China has become the first or second most important market for almost all the countries in the region. This development has led those who view economic relations through a nation-state lens to believe that China's rapid, import-dependent growth has made it possible for the region to "uncouple" from the U.S. economy, thereby avoiding

TABLE 1.5: Share of Parts and Components in Manufacturing Trade, 1992/3 and 2006/7 (percent)

| | TOTAL TRADE | | | | INTRAREGIONAL TRADE | | | |
	exports		imports		exports		imports	
	1992/3	2006/7	1992/3	2006/7	1992/3	2006/7	1992/3	2006/7
Developing Asia	17.3	34.0	29.0	44.2	21.6	53.9	32.9	59.5
PRC	7.4	25.6	20.4	44.0	9.4	40.6	23.7	59.2
Hong Kong, China	15.8	33.3	24.1	48.5	17.2	58.3	35.7	60.1
Taiwan	24.7	44.2	29.5	38.9	25.3	50.5	39.4	58.3
Korea, Rep. of	18.1	47.3	30.1	31.9	21.0	63.5	38.8	38.1
Malaysia	27.7	53.6	40.5	50.0	39.8	74.5	47.9	53.7
Philippines	32.9	71.7	32.6	61.3	47.2	99.6	38.6	65.8
Singapore	29.0	49.3	39.9	60.4	41.6	68.5	47.2	64.8
Thailand	14.1	29.9	30.6	36.1	20.2	41.5	36.2	38.7
East Asia	20.2	34.1	27.2	42.1	24.9	50.1	30.3	52.8
Japan	23.9	34.4	19.3	29.9	28.9	42.0	19.3	34.2
NAFTA	28.4	31.2	37.4	28.8	20.9	28.8	47.6	36.3
EU15	18.3	22.4	21.2	23.2	18.4	22.0	20.5	22.1
World	19.3	27.1	19.6	27.3	NA	NA	NA	NA

Source: Perma-chandra, "Asian Trade Flows: Trends, Patterns, and Projections," Asian Development Bank, Economics Working Paper No. 2009/15, January 2011, 17.

the consequences of U.S. economic problems. However, since the region's trade activity largely involves an intraregional trade of parts and components culminating in China-based exports aimed primarily at the United States and the European Union, the reality is that Asia has become ever more tightly integrated and dependent on exporting to developed capitalist markets, especially the United States.

This outcome is illustrated by the following trends: the correlation between the growth in East Asian exports and U.S. non-oil imports rose from .21 during the 1980s to .34 during the 1990s, and .77 during the first half of the 2000s.[52] Even more revealing is that the correlation between East Asian intraregional exports and U.S. non-oil imports increased from .01 during the 1980s to .22 during the 1990s, and .63 during the first half of the 2000s.[53] Thus, as a consequence of transnational capital's accumulation dynamics, external demand rather than regional need has become the primary driver of East Asian economic activity.

Global Imbalances and Instabilities

Though the internationalization of production has been a profitable strategy for transnational capital, it has also generated enormous trade imbalances that are increasingly unsustainable. At its core, the internationalization of production is an export-oriented strategy and the ever-expanding scale of transnational production requires ever-expanding external markets to absorb the output. The poles of the created imbalance are currently China, which serves as the primary production hub, and the United States, which serves as the primary consumer of the goods produced.

Table 1.6 highlights the critical role played by the United States as the world's major consumer of imported goods. The size of the U.S. deficit as a percentage of world GDP grew steadily from 1997 to 2006, counterbalancing the large surpluses of China, Japan, and the rest of East Asia. In 2006, the United States accounted for

TABLE 1.6: World Current Account Balance (Percent World GDP)

Year	U.S.	Russian Fed.	Middle East	Japan	People's Rep. China	Rest of Dev. Asia	Other Indus. Countries	Rest of World
1985	-0.99		0.00	0.43	-0.10	0.02	0.04	-0.08
1986	-1.05		-0.08	0.61	-0.05	0.11	0.19	-0.29
1987	-1.00		-0.03	0.52	0.00	0.16	0.07	-0.19
1988	-0.67		-0.03	0.44	-0.02	0.11	-0.07	-0.17
1989	-0.52		0.00	0.33	-0.02	0.06	-0.15	-0.20
1990	-0.37		0.03	0.21	0.06	-0.03	-0.21	-0.18
1991	0.01		-0.29	0.31	0.06	-0.04	-0.45	-0.19
1992	-0.21	0.00	-0.10	0.46	0.03	-0.02	-0.40	-0.24
1993	-0.34	0.01	-0.08	0.53	-0.05	-0.01	-0.15	-0.17
1994	-0.46	0.03	-0.02	0.49	0.03	-0.05	-0.12	-0.14
1995	-0.38	0.02	0.02	0.38	0.01	-0.13	-0.06	-0.06
1996	-0.41	0.04	0.06	0.22	0.02	-0.16	0.13	-0.05
1997	-0.46	0.00	0.04	0.32	0.12	-0.08	0.17	-0.12
1998	-0.72	0.00	-0.08	0.40	0.10	0.26	0.10	-0.35
1999	-0.96	0.08	0.05	0.37	0.05	0.25	-0.02	-0.21
2000	-1.30	0.15	0.22	0.37	0.06	0.19	-0.12	-0.14
2001	-1.24	0.11	0.13	0.27	0.05	0.21	0.03	-0.11
2002	-1.38	0.09	0.08	0.34	0.11	0.26	0.10	-0.01
2003	-1.39	0.09	0.14	0.36	0.12	0.32	0.05	0.11
2004	-1.50	0.14	0.22	0.41	0.16	0.25	0.24	0.07
2005	-1.64	0.19	0.43	0.36	0.35	0.19	0.14	0.05
2006	-1.63	0.19	0.53	0.35	0.51	0.27	0.13	0.08
2007	-1.29	0.14	0.45	0.38	0.67	0.29	0.21	-0.29
2008	-1.09	0.17	0.53	0.26	0.71	0.18	0.12	-0.53
2009	-0.65	0.09	0.11	0.25	0.51	0.28	-0.03	-0.18

Source: Asian Development Bank, *Asian Development Outlook 2011* (Philippines: Asian Development Bank, 2011), 3.

roughly 50 percent of aggregate current account deficits in the world economy while China accounted for roughly 22 percent of aggregate current account surpluses.[54]

Transnational capital's adoption of a cross-border production strategy based in East Asia has transformed the U.S.-China trade relationship. The value of U.S. imports from China increased from $16 billion in 1990 to $340 billion in 2007. In 2003, China became the world's second-largest exporter to the United States, trailing only Canada. The position of these two countries has fluctuated since, with China becoming the largest exporter in 2007 and then again in 2009. U.S. exports to China have also grown, but far more slowly, increasing from $5 billion in 1990 to $65 billion in 2007. As a consequence, the U.S. trade deficit with China grew dramatically, from $11 billion in 1990 to $274 billion in 2007. This was the largest deficit that the United States had with any country.[55]

Though the overwhelming majority of U.S. imports from China have long been manufactures (approximately 96 percent), their composition, in line with China's evolving assembly role, has changed over time. The share of "miscellaneous" manufactures, such as toys, clothes, and footwear, fell from 58.5 percent in 1995–96 to 37.7 percent in 2005–6. Over the same period, the import share of machinery and transportation equipment products rose from 26.3 percent to 44.1 percent. Within this broad category, ICT products dominate. In 2005–6, they made up 37.6 percent of all U.S. manufactured imports from China. Not only have Chinese imports to the United States become increasingly sophisticated, China is increasingly the main foreign supplier of such products. For example, China's share of total U.S. ICT imports rose from 6.5 percent in 1995–96 to 33 percent in 2005–6.[56]

These trends highlight the reason that Chinese exports receive so much attention in the United States. However, as we have seen, these "sophisticated" Chinese exports are Chinese only in the sense that they were assembled in China. This point is reinforced by the fact that China's increased share of the U.S. trade deficit was matched by a decline in the share accounted for by the rest of East Asia. From 1999 to 2007, China's share of the total U.S. trade deficit rose from 20.4 percent to 32.1 percent. Over the same period, Japan's share fell from 21.1 percent to 10.2 percent. And the combined share of the rest of East Asia also fell, from 16 percent to 7.9 percent.[57]

East Asia's China-centered export-driven growth has also had important ripple effects outside the region. Most directly, it has translated into a booming demand for critical primary commodities, pushing up their prices to the benefit of many commodity-exporting nations in Latin America and Sub-Saharan Africa.[58] As *The Economist* noted, "China's appetite for raw materials is particularly voracious because of the country's size and its high investment rate. Though it accounts for only about one-eighth of global output, China uses up between a third and half of the world's annual production of iron ore, aluminium, lead and other non-precious metals."[59] China's resource needs have also led it to engage in significant mining, natural gas, and oil investments in both Latin America and Sub-Saharan Africa.[60]

In other words, U.S. trade deficits have fueled not only East Asian growth but also (indirectly) Latin American and Sub-Saharan African growth. As explained in the *Trade and Development Report 2010*: "The three main developments [shaping global growth] since the beginning of the millennium were: the decline in national savings and the rapid increase in household consumption in the United States; the growing importance of investment and exports for growth in large Asian developing countries, particularly China; and the unprecedented surge in the prices of primary commodities after 2002."[61]

Thus, the world economy has become increasingly dependent not just on U.S. growth in general, but on U.S. household consumption. In the years before the Great Recession, U.S. household consumption was directly responsible for approximately 16 percent of world output with imports constituting a major share.[62] According to the *Trade and Development Report 2010*:

From 2000 to 2007, United States imports as a share of its GDP grew from 15 percent to 17 percent, boosting aggregate demand in the rest of the world by $937 billion, in nominal terms. Moreover, as a result of global production sharing, United States consumer spending increases global economic activities in many indirect ways as well (e.g., business investments in countries such as Germany and Japan to produce machinery for export to China and its use there for the manufacture of exports to the United States).[63]

This global dependence on U.S. household consumption highlights the fragility of contemporary international growth dynamics. Personal U.S. consumption as a share of GDP grew rapidly beginning in the late 1990s from its long-term average of approximately 66 percent to over 70 percent in 2007. This growth was largely financed by household borrowing made possible by a skyrocketing housing bubble; the ratio of debt to personal disposable income reached an all-time high in 2007, exceeding 130 percent.[64] With stagnant wage and private sector job growth, households had little choice but to rely on debt to finance their consumption. And with business spending on plants and equipment constrained because of a lack of perceived profitable investment opportunities, the U.S. government was more than willing to encourage the increasingly speculative financialization process that underpinned the country's economic expansion. The eventual collapse of the housing bubble and the resulting financial crisis has brought this process to a halt, leaving the U.S. economy facing a future of stagnation with limited consumption growth.[65]

There is no other country capable of replacing the United States. Annual U.S. household consumption averaged almost $10 trillion over 2007–8. In Japan, household consumption averaged only $2.5 trillion. In Germany, it was less than $2 trillion.[66] Moreover, both Japan and Germany are committed to an export-led growth strategy, which requires their governments to suppress wage growth and, by extension, consumption spending. China, despite its rapid economic growth, is also not a viable replacement. Its consumption is only one-eighth that of the United States. In addition, "The import content of domestic consumption in China is less than 8 percent—three times smaller than in the United States."[67]

To this point, U.S. economic difficulties have not triggered a worldwide downturn. Perhaps the main reason is that China has maintained its own rapid growth in the face of declining exports thanks to a massive state program of investment, especially in roads, bridges, high-speed rail, and airports; investment as a share of GDP has risen from 39.1 percent in 2007 to an astounding 46.2 percent in 2010. China's growth has, in turn, limited the decline in economic activity in East Asia. And, by supporting commodity prices, it has also helped maintain growth in Latin America and Sub-Saharan Africa. In 2009, Chinese demand for the main base metals (aluminum, copper, lead, nickel, tin, and zinc) increased by 23 percent, while demand fell by 13.5 percent in the rest of the world.[68]

However, there are clear signs that Chinese state policies are not sustainable. Many of China's infrastructure investments are of dubious economic or social value, and serious questions are being raised about whether the local governments that borrowed to undertake them will be able to repay their debts. State industries that expanded their capacity to participate in these projects are also facing serious overcapacity challenges. Both developments threaten the stability of the country's financial system. Finally, the central government's low-interest-rate policy, which played a critical role in supporting the investment binge, has also triggered a housing bubble that appears dangerously close to bursting.[69]

In short, it appears that Chinese state policies have only delayed the wrenching adjustments that await most of the countries of East Asia, Latin America, and Sub-Saharan Africa. In fact, as Michael Pettis explains:

This delayed transmission [of the crisis to the third world], by the way, is not new. It also happened in the mid-1970s with the petrodollar recycling. Economic contraction in the

United States and Europe in the early and mid-1970s did not lead immediately to economic contraction in what were then known as LDCs [Less Developed Countries], largely because the massive recycling of petrodollar surpluses into the developing world fueled an investment boom (and also fueled talk about how for the first time in history the LDCs were immune from rich-country recessions). When the investment boom ran out in 1980–81, driven by the debt fatigue that seems to end all major investment booms, LDCs suffered the "Lost Decade" of the 1980s, especially those who suffered least in the 1970s by running up the most debt.

    This time around a huge recycling of liquidity, combined with out-of-control Chinese fiscal expansion (through the banking system), has caused a surge in asset and commodity prices that will have temporarily masked the impact of global demand contraction for BRIC [Brazil, Russia, India, and China]. But it won't last. By the middle of this decade the whole concept of BRIC decoupling will seem faintly ridiculous.[70]

The negative consequences of contemporary capitalist accumulation dynamics are not limited to the unbalanced and unstable global production and consumption patterns they created. Equally important, while these dynamics greatly benefited transnational corporations and their national allies, they were enormously costly for working-class majorities in the countries most directly affected by them. To show how this happened, it is necessary to examine the causes and consequences of the connected economic transformations of China and the United States, the primary anchors of contemporary capitalist accumulation.

Globalization and the Chinese Experience

The process by which the Chinese economy became the linchpin of East Asia's regional production system is a complex one. In 1978, two years after the death of Mao Zedong, the Chinese Communist Party (CCP) decided to radically increase the economy's reliance on market forces. The reforms soon led to the privileging of markets over planning and private ownership over public ownership. They also generated serious banking, fiscal, and trade problems as well as social tensions. In response, the CCP took steps to encourage transnational corporate investment, hoping that it would stabilize the banking sector, boost state revenues, increase exports, and promote job growth. In this way, although unplanned, the Chinese economy became enmeshed in transnational capital's cross-border production networks.[71]

As a consequence, China's growth has become increasingly dependent on exports produced by transnational corporations. The country's export-to-GDP ratio rose dramatically from 8 percent in the early 1980s to 18 percent in the early 1990s, 28 percent in the early 2000s, and 36 percent in 2007. Yilmaz Aklyuz, using input-output data to isolate the value added contribution of China's export activity to the country's growth, found it to be substantial:

> The evidence suggests that in recent years [2004–7] the average import content of Chinese exports has been between 40 and 50 percent; that is, domestic value-added generated by exports is less than 60 percent of their gross value. In value-added terms the share of exports in GDP is in the order of 20 percent. . . .
>
> Despite high import content of exports, one-third of growth of income in China in the years before the outbreak of the global crisis is estimated to have been due to exports because of their phenomenal growth of 25 percent per annum. This figure goes up to 40 percent if spillovers to domestic consumption (the multiplier) are accounted for and to 50 percent with knock-on effects on domestic investment.[72]

This high export contribution is confirmed by Andong Zhu and David M. Kotz who find that "China's rapid growth was initially based on its domestic market, specifically rising consumption by

TABLE 1.7: Export Growth Performance of TNCs in China

Year	Total Export Growth Rate	Share of TNCs in Exports	TNC Export Growth Rate	Export Growth Rate without TNCs
1991	15.80	16.70	53.90	6.82
1992	18.10	20.50	45.00	8.90
1993	8.00	27.50	44.90	-4.32
1994	31.90	28.40	36.40	21.56
1995	22.90	31.50	36.40	11.49
1996	1.50	40.70	31.10	-11.13
1997	21.00	41.00	21.90	12.03
1998	0.50	44.10	8.00	-3.03
1999	6.10	45.50	9.50	1.81
2000	27.80	47.90	34.70	11.20
2001	6.80	50.10	11.60	0.99
2002	22.40	52.20	27.50	7.99
2003	34.60	54.80	41.40	11.91
2004	35.40	57.10	41.10	11.96

Source: John Whalley and Xian Xin, "China's FDI and non-FDI Economies and the Sustainability of Future High Chinese Growth," National Bureau of Economic Research, paper no. 122249, May 2006, 6.

households and government. However, since 2001 exports have played a major role in China's growth, along with fixed investment."[73] More specifically, they concluded that value added exports—the value of exports minus the value of all the imported inputs directly or indirectly used in the production of exported goods and services—accounted for approximately 12 percent of China's growth in the period 1978 to 1988, but 32 percent of its growth in the period 2001 to 2007.[74] These percentages do not include any spillover effects of Chinese export activity in the country's consumption or investment.

A National Bureau of Economic Research study of the TNC contribution to China's growth, which included the consequences of national as well as export-directed activity, concluded that TNCs were responsible for approximately 30 percent of China's growth over the period 1995 to 2004, with the share rising to over 40 percent in 2003 and 2004.[75] In particular, the authors noted, "Since 1990 [TNCs] have accounted for most of China's export growth."[76] As Table 1.7 shows, the TNC share of China's exports increased from 16.7 percent in 1991 to 57.1 percent in 2004.

As discussed above, transnational cross-border production networks are heavily focused on the production and export of high-technology goods. Not surprisingly, then, transnational corporations have turned China into a major exporter of these goods. In 1995, China's high-technology exports amounted to $10.1 billion, only 6.8 percent of total exports. The country's world market share was only 2.1 percent. From 1995 to 2009, high-tech exports grew 30 percent annually, considerably faster than growth in overall exports. In 2009, China's high-technology exports reached $376.9 billion, equal to 31.4 percent of total exports. In 2006, China became the world's largest exporter of high-technology goods with a market share of 16.9 percent.[77]

The leading role of transnational corporations is highlighted by the fact that they produce approximately 85 percent of China's high-technology exports. Moreover, the share of China's high-technology exports produced by wholly owned transnational corporations continues to grow, from 55 percent in 2002 to 68 percent in 2009, suggesting a tightening of foreign control.[78] This dominance is perhaps best illustrated by an examination of Chinese computer exports, one of the country's leading high-technology exports.

China is the world's number one exporter of computers. Yet China's contribution to this activity is limited to providing cheap labor and land. China's top export position is due to the fact that Taiwanese original design manufacturers (ODMs)—who dominate worldwide computer manufacturing—have shifted their production of laptops and desktops, as well as motherboards and monitors, to the mainland (see Table 1.8). For example, in 2001, Taiwanese computer makers manufactured only 4 percent of their laptop computers in China. Five years later, it was 96.8 percent.

As a result of this shift, eight of China's top ten exporters are now Taiwanese ODMs that supply "branded PC sellers such as Dell with unbranded computers and components. . . . There are no Chinese ODMs and there are no significant Chinese suppliers to the Taiwanese ODMs, or to their suppliers."[79]

Much like the previously discussed examples of the iPhone and iPad, China's limited production role in the export of computers means that its gains from the export of computers are also limited. As Yuqing Xing explains:

> In 2009, [China] exported 108.5 million laptop PCs with an average selling price US$484 per unit. The total laptop PC exports amounted to US$52.5 billion, about 14 percent of total high-tech exports.
>
> Dedrick, Kraemer and Linden estimated that assembly represents 3 percent of the entire manufacturing cost of a laptop PC. Using this estimate as a reference, the value added per laptop PC by Chinese workers would be US$14.5 and China's laptop PC export in terms of the value added would be US$1.6 billion, much lower than indicated by conventional trade statistics.[80]

In sum, China's rise as an export powerhouse is primarily due to its position as the final assembly platform for transnational corporate cross-border production networks. This point is reinforced by *Businessweek*, which noted that "experts familiar with highly touted Chinese achievements such as commercial jets and high-speed trains say the technologies that underpin them were largely developed elsewhere." China may be the world's leading exporter of high-technology products, "but subtract the mainland operations of Taiwanese contract manufacturers and the likes of Nokia, Samsung, and Hewlett-Packard, and China is an electronics lightweight."[81]

In highlighting the leading role of TNCs in China's widely celebrated export success I do not mean to suggest that this export

TABLE 1.8: Shares of IT Products Made in China by Taiwanese TNCs

Year	Laptop PC	Desktop PC	Motherboard	LCD Monitor for PC
2003	54.3	51.7	73.9	79.1
2004	77.8	54.1	86.2	84.6
2005	92.8	57.5	91.6	88.7
2006	96.9	63.9	94.0	90.6
2007	97.8	71.7	96.4	91.5

Source: Yuqing Xing, "China's High-Tech Exports: Myth and Reality, "EAI Background Brief 506," East Asia Institute, National University of Singapore, February 2010, 12.

activity fully captures the Chinese experience. In particular, the Chinese state remains a significant force in shaping Chinese economic activity, which includes but is not limited to the promotion of foreign direct investment. Moreover, an increasingly wealthy Chinese elite has developed through its ties to transnational corporate organized production and, more important, Chinese state-owned enterprises, which dominate in several strategic sectors, including finance, transportation, oil, petrochemicals, power generation, and telecommunications. At the same time, China's rise to become the world's dominant producer and exporter of manufactures and the process generating current global trade imbalances cannot be understood in isolation from the broader regional restructuring shaped by transnational corporate investment.[82]

Despite China's new economic status, the restructuring of its economy has come at high cost. As we have seen, China's high-technology export activity contributes little to Chinese national development. Indeed, China's participation in transnational production networks tends to limit the country's own technological development and industrial diversification.

Such an outcome is not surprising. A United Nations Conference on Trade and Development (UNCTAD) study found that "participating in international production chains" often leaves the host country "locked into its current structure of comparative advantage

. . . thereby delaying the exploitation of potential comparative advantage in higher-tech stages of production." These limitations have been "causing concern in recent years, even in some of the East Asian countries that have been more successful in exploiting various advantages associated with TNCs."[83] UNCTAD highlights several reasons for such concern. Among the most important:

> The spillovers from engaging in subcontracting or hosting affiliates of TNCs are reduced because the package of technology and skills required at any one site becomes narrower and because cross-border backward and forward linkages are strengthened at the expense of domestic ones. Furthermore, when only a small part of the production chain is involved, out-contractors and TNCs have a wider choice of potential sites—since these activities take on a more footloose character—which strengthens their bargaining position vis-à-vis the host country. This can engender excessive and unhealthy competition among developing countries as they begin to offer TNCs increasing fiscal and trade-related concessions in order to compensate for the shifting competitiveness from one group of developing countries to another; it can thereby aggravate the inequalities in the distribution of gains from international trade and investment between TNCs and developing countries.[84]

The social costs of economic restructuring have been far greater. For example, China's rapid export-led growth has failed to generate adequate employment opportunities for Chinese workers. According to the U.S. Bureau of Labor Statistics, total manufacturing employment in China actually fell by almost 7 million over the period 1994–2006, from 119.26 million to 112.63 million (see Table 1.9). Total urban manufacturing employment, which includes most foreign operations, declined sharply from 54.92 million to 33.52 million. Though this decline was partially offset by an expansion in rural manufacturing employment, rural

TABLE 1.9: Manufacturing Employment in China, 1994-2006 (mill.)

Year	Total Manufacturing Employment in Urban Units	Total Manufacturing Employment in Township and Village Enterprises (TVEs)	Total Manufacturing Employment
1994	54.92	64.34	119.26
1995	54.93	69.92	124.85
1996	53.44	72.64	126.08
1997	51.30	56.83	108.13
1998	38.26	67.78	106.04
1999	35.54	68.35	103.89
2000	33.01	69.01	102.02
2001	30.70	70.38	101.08
2002	29.81	70.87	100.68
2003	29.81	72.73	102.54
2004	30.51	75.68	106.19
2005	32.11	78.48	110.59
2006	33.52	79.11	112.63

Source: Erin Lett and Judith Banister, "China's Manufacturing Employment and Compensation Costs: 2002–06," *Monthly Labor Review*, April 2009, 32.

manufacturing workers are paid far less and are subject to far worse workplace conditions than urban manufacturing workers.[85]

Actually, China's growth has generated few decent employment opportunities for urban workers, regardless of their employment sector. An International Labor Organization study of urban employment found that although total urban employment increased slightly over the period 1990 to 2002, almost all the growth was in irregular employment, meaning casual-wage or self-employment—typically in construction, cleaning and maintenance of premises, retail trade, street vending, repair services, or domestic services. More specifically, while total urban employment over this thirteen-year period grew by 81.7 million, 80 million of that growth was in irregular employment.[86] As a result, irregular workers in China now constitute the largest single urban employment category. This growing informalization of employment parallels developments in Latin America and Sub-Saharan Africa, areas where (in contrast to China) capitalist accumulation was said to be stagnant.

Above all, Chinese labor policies have been designed to attract foreign investment and boost the export competitiveness of firms operating in China. Wage and consumption trends provide one measure of their success. Chinese wages as a share of GDP fell from approximately 53 percent of GDP in 1992 to below 40 percent in 2006. Private consumption as a percent of GDP also declined, falling from approximately 47 percent to 36 percent over the same period. As *The Economist* pointed out, "The decline in the ratio of consumption to GDP . . . is largely explained by a sharp drop in the share of national income going to households (in the form of wages, government transfers and investment income), while the shares of profits and government revenues have risen. . . . Many countries have seen a fall in the share of labor income in recent years, but nowhere has the drop been as huge as in China."[87]

Strikingly, the consumption share of GDP has continued to fall, to a low of 33.8 percent in 2010.[88] Pettis highlights just how low this is by noting that "household consumption in the rest of the world tends to be around 65 percent of GDP. For the group of Asian countries that followed the Japanese growth model and so repressed consumption to achieve high growth rates, household consumption typically clocked in at 50–55 percent of GDP."[89] A vicious cycle is at work: the lower the share of income going to workers and by extension consumption, the more economic forces reinforce the export orientation of the Chinese economy, thereby encouraging the Chinese state to support policies that further suppress worker wages.

Chinese state policies toward internal migrants have been critical to the achievement of state aims. Internal migrants make up approximately 70 percent of the country's manufacturing workforce and 80 percent of its construction workforce. Over the last twenty-five years, some 150–200 million Chinese have moved from the countryside to urban areas in search of employment. Although the great majority moved legally, they remain classified as rural residents under the Chinese registration system and thus suffer enormous discrimination. For example, despite paying fees to register as temporary urban residents, they are denied access to the public services available to urban-born residents (including free or subsidized education, health care, housing, and pensions). The same is true for their children, even if they are born in an urban area.[90]

As a result, migrant workers are easily exploitable. Most work 11 hours a day, 26 days a month, and receive no special overtime pay.[91] According to a U.S. Bureau of Labor Statistics study, average hourly compensation (wages and benefits) for manufacturing workers in China in 2006 was 81 cents, significantly less than that paid in the Philippines or Mexico and only 2.7 percent of the U.S. average.[92] Although several strong years of wage growth have pushed up Chinese manufacturing wages, they still remain low. A 2011 study by the All China Federation of Trade Unions found that the new generation of migrant workers employed in manufacturing, those born after 1980 but also over 16 years of age, earned an average monthly salary of approximately $270, which, given the typical length of the work week, was the equivalent of approximately 90 cents an hour.[93]

At the same time, a report on labor practices in China by Verite Inc., a U.S. company that advises transnational corporations on responsible business practices, found that "systemic problems in payment practices in Chinese export business practices consistently rob workers of at least 15 percent of their pay."[94] Workplace safety is an even greater problem. According to official Chinese government sources, about 200 million workers labor under "hazardous" conditions: "Every year there are more than 700,000 serious work-related injuries nation-wide, claiming 130,000 lives."[95]

A 2010 China Labor Watch investigation into labor conditions at 46 factories (employing a total of 92,000 workers) in Guangdong and Jiangsu provinces found the following:

A) The ability for workers to organize and express their griev-
   ances is extremely limited, and poses a serious problem. In
   88.2 percent of the surveyed factories, there was no functional
   or effective trade union or grievance mechanism system.

B) In 87 percent of the factories, daily overtime work
   exceeded three hours or there was no guarantee of one day
   of rest each week. Not one factory met the legal requirements for overtime monthly maximum of 36 hours. In the
   surveyed factories, overtime hours in excess of 100 hours
   was the norm, and some were even in excess of 200 hours.

C) 82.6 percent of the factories surveyed do not pay wages in
   accordance with Chinese labor laws, with regard to minimum wage and/or overtime rates. As workers have no
   means of engaging in collective bargaining, there is little
   hope of wage increases.[96]

It is not just low wages that attract transnational corporations
to China, it is also the broader work environment, an environment that offers corporations maximum freedom to mobilize and
direct the work effort of their employees.[97] The *New York Times*,
in discussing why Apple relies on China-based production for its
products, offered the following story:

> One former [Apple] executive described how the company
> relied upon a Chinese factory to revamp iPhone manufactur-
> ing just weeks before the device was due on shelves. Apple
> had redesigned the iPhone's screen at the last minute, forcing
> an assembly line overhaul. New screens began arriving at the
> plant near midnight.
>
> A foreman immediately roused 8,000 workers inside the
> company's dormitories, according to the executive. Each
> employee was given a biscuit and a cup of tea, guided to a
> workstation and within half an hour started a 12-hour shift
> fitting glass screens into beveled frames. Within 96 hours, the
> plant was producing over 10,000 iPhones a day.

"The speed and flexibility is breathtaking," the executive said.[98]

The social costs of transnational capital's current accumulation dynamics are not limited to China. Because of the country's key position in East Asia's cross-border production networks, Chinese conditions generally serve as the benchmark by which transnational corporations evaluate the economic environment in other countries. Thus countries throughout East Asia have become pitted against each other in what appears to be a losing effort to match what is available in China. A case in point: the ratio of investment to GDP fell sharply throughout all of East Asia in the aftermath of the 1997–98 regional crisis. However, as the Asian Development Bank reported, there has been little or no improvement in the following years:

> Investment as a share of GDP across the region has been unusually low since the Asian crisis. In countries in which there had been massive overinvestment in real estate during the lead-up to the crisis, the real estate sector tends to account for a significant share of overall investment weakness; this is understandable since a return to lower, more sustainable investment rates would be expected. For the most part, however, investment weakness has occurred across all components of investment, both in countries that were at the center of the crisis and those that were not [with China, India, and Vietnam the only exceptions].[99]

In response to China's success in attracting investment and boosting export activity, governments throughout the region have introduced new labor regimes designed to weaken labor protections. As a consequence, wages and working conditions have also worsened throughout the region.[100] Among other things, this dynamic works to reinforce the bias of the entire region toward exports, thereby intensifying the structural nature of the imbalances highlighted above.

South Korea provides a good illustration of how countries in the region have been negatively affected by transnational corporate accumulation dynamics. Its investment as a share of GDP fell from an average of over 37 percent during the period 1990 to 1997, to less than 30 percent from 2000 to 2007.[101] South Korean government efforts to boost investment, especially foreign direct investment, have largely been unsuccessful. A major reason is that China offers a more attractive location. In 2004, the head of the American Chamber of Commerce in Korea made this explicit when he said, "Korea's competition is Shanghai, Hong Kong and China. Realize what your competition is, because investors can choose where to go." He singled out the need for more "labor flexibility."[102] South Korean transnational corporations have also been shifting investment and production to China. As a result of these combined investment trends, net foreign direct investment actually recorded an outflow of almost $1 billion in the first half of 2008, the first negative total since data collection on FDI began in 1980.[103]

As South Korea has become further integrated into transnational capital's cross-border production strategy, its growth has also become increasingly dependent on exports, with China the leading destination. China now takes over 30 percent of South Korean exports. Approximately 70 percent of these exports are intermediate products that receive further processing and are then re-exported as Chinese exports.[104] One measure of South Korea's current dependence on China-based economic activity: net exports to China (including Hong Kong) accounted for 52 percent of South Korea's growth between the first half of 2008 and the first half of 2010.[105]

South Korea's restructuring has come at great cost to its workers and their families. Poverty rates soared from approximately 9 percent in 1996 to 20 percent in 2006. Inequality has also hit record levels: the top 20 percent income bracket earned 4.5 times more than the bottom 20 percent in 1996 and 7.1 times more in 2006.[106] Labor market restructuring is perhaps the major cause of these negative social trends. The percentage of workers with irregular labor status has grown from approximately 40 percent before 2000 to over 60 percent by 2008. These workers generally earn only a little more than half of what regular workers earn in monthly wages.[107] In sum, capitalist accumulation, even in East Asia, the world's most dynamic production location, offers working people few benefits.

Globalization and the U.S. Experience

The United States, like China, also underwent a major economic transformation beginning in the late 1970s. As previously discussed, U.S. corporations responded to profit pressures with increased foreign direct investment. This trend was reinforced by the adoption of a similar strategy by rival transnational corporations, especially those headquartered in Japan. U.S. government efforts to restore competitiveness through attacks on the U.S. working class succeeded in driving down wages and working conditions but did little to rejuvenate the manufacturing sector. The U.S. trade deficit as a percentage of GDP grew steadily, from –0.9 in 1980, to –1.9 in 1990, –4.2 in 2001, and –5.9 in 2007.

The combination of declining wages and the growing trade deficit led to the rise of finance as the country's dominant corporate sector. The decline in wages encouraged household borrowing, boosting the profitability of the financial sector. Finance received an even greater boost from growing capital inflows, the flipside of the ever-growing U.S. trade deficit.

However, economic growth remained weak until the mid-1990s, when a series of bubbles, first in the stock market and then in the housing market, pushed up household wealth and touched off a massive consumption boom. The housing bubble alone increased wealth by some $8 trillion by 2006.[108] With median income declining over the period, households financed their consumption by borrowing, using their new housing wealth as collateral.

Household debt doubled from $7 trillion to $14 trillion between 2000 and 2007, with housing-related debt responsible for 80 percent of the increase. In 2007, the household debt-to-GDP ratio reached its highest level since 1929.[109] Not surprisingly given this pattern of economic activity, the financial sector's share of total corporate profits grew from less than 20 percent in the late 1960s to approximately 40 percent before the start of the financial crisis.[110]

The collapse of the housing bubble wiped out household wealth as well as the value of many loans and financial assets, which were based on housing values. The result was the Great Recession in the United States. The post-crisis recovery has been one of the weakest on record, largely because consumer spending remains limited by a continuing debt overhang and high rates of unemployment.

The contradictory nature of contemporary capitalist accumulation dynamics is highlighted by the fact that these dynamics simultaneously created an East Asian–centered production system organized to export to the United States as it weakened the purchasing power of U.S. workers, thereby making it difficult for them to play their assigned role as preeminent consumers. The significance of this contradiction was masked for approximately a decade because of the rise of speculative bubbles in the United States. Now that these bubbles have burst, the structural imbalances and instabilities generated by capitalist globalization have become increasingly apparent.

One way to appreciate how the above described internationalization of production has weakened U.S. workers' purchasing power is to study its effects on U.S. labor markets. David H. Autor, David Dorn, and Gordon H. Hanson made the case for carefully considering the connection between Chinese export activity and U.S. labor market conditions:

> One factor limiting trade's impact on U.S. labor is that, historically, imports from low-wage countries have been small. Though freer trade with countries at any income level may affect wages and employment, trade theory identifies

low-wage countries as a likely source of disruption to high-wage labor markets. In 1991, low-income countries accounted for just 2.9 percent of U.S. manufacturing imports. However, owing largely to China's spectacular growth, the situation has changed markedly. In 2000, the low-income-country share of U.S. imports reached 5.9 percent and climbed to 11.7 percent by 2007, with China accounting for 91.5 percent of this import growth over the period.[111]

Autor, Dorn, and Hanson investigated the effect of imports from China on U.S. employment and wages between 1990 and 2007. They first divided the U.S. mainland into 727 regional labor markets based on defined "commuting zones" (CZs). Next, they estimated the share of Chinese exports to the United States that were due to rising Chinese competitiveness rather than changes in U.S. market demand. They did this by correlating the growth and composition of Chinese exports to the United States with the growth and composition of Chinese exports to eight other developed capitalist countries.

The authors then classified these Chinese exports by industry and, assuming that they represented competition for U.S. producers, apportioned them year by year to each CZ according to its share of national employment in the relevant industry. Finally, they estimated the relationship between changes in Chinese import exposure per worker in each CZ and changes in CZ employment and wages.

Autor, Dorn, and Hanson determined that a "conservative estimate [is] that Chinese import competition explains 16 percent of the U.S. manufacturing employment decline between 1991 and 2000, 28 percent of the decline between 2000 and 2007, and 23 percent of the decline over the full period."[112] And these estimates do not include potentially lost employment from Chinese competition in third-country markets. Despite the loss of manufacturing employment, the authors found no evidence that Chinese import competition lowered average manufacturing wages.

They did find that this import competition reduced both employment and earnings in sectors outside of manufacturing. Apparently, the loss of manufacturing work reduced the demand for local non-traded services and thus non-manufacturing employment. At the same time, the loss of manufacturing work swelled the supply of non-manufacturing workers, putting downward pressure on non-manufacturing wages. Overall, they concluded, the combination of falling employment and declining wage levels had significantly negative effects on "the level and composition of household income in local labor markets exposed to growing Chinese import competition. The estimates . . . find that a $1,000 increase in a CZ's import exposure leads to a fall in CZ average household wage and salary income per working age adult of . . . about $549 per working age adult and year."[113]

Of course, the internationalization of production cannot simply be reduced to China-based export activity. The transformation of the U.S. economy has been shaped by a multiplicity of operations involving both foreign and U.S. transnational corporations operating in many parts of the world. For example, many transnational corporations, U.S. ones in particular, have taken advantage of NAFTA to establish production networks in Mexico and Canada that are also aimed at the U.S. market. Thus Autor, Dorn, and Hanson's work must be taken as only suggestive of the economic costs imposed on U.S. workers by capitalist globalization dynamics.

Michael Spence and Sandile Hlatshwayo's study of trends in U.S. employment and value added in both tradeable and non-tradeable sectors from 1990 to 2008 provides additional insight into the ways in which the U.S. economy has been transformed by capitalist globalization and the costs of that transformation.[114] They began by dividing U.S. industries and their sub-industries into tradeable and non-tradeable sectors using a geographic concentration index. That index measured "the tradability of an industry based on its geographic concentration—the more concentrated the industry, the higher its tradability (and vice versa)." They then "adapted and adjusted their classifications by critically looking at each industry's tradability estimate and using both common sense and export and import data to see whether their proportions reflect industries' international tradability."[115]

Starting with employment, the authors found that almost all job growth from 1990 to 2008 occurred in the non-tradeable sector. Specifically, there was a 27.3 million increase in total employment between 1990 and 2008, from a starting base of 121.9 million. Approximately 98 percent of that increase, 26.7 million jobs, was generated in the non-tradeable sector. Overall job creation in the tradeable sector was basically nonexistent.[116]

In 2008, the non-tradeable sector had 114.9 million jobs and the tradeable sector 34.3 million jobs. Government at all levels was the largest employer in the non-tradable sector, with 22.5 million jobs. Health care was second, with 16.3 million. In terms of job growth over the period, health care generated the most new jobs, followed by government, with increases of 6.3 million and 4.1 million respectively. These two sectors together combined for approximately 40 percent of total employment gains. The other large job-creating sectors were retail, accommodation and food service, and construction. In 2008, these five accounted for 73.5 million jobs or approximately 50 percent of total gains.[117]

Ominously, employment in both government and health care depends heavily on public spending. Current austerity trends threaten to limit employment growth in these sectors, foreshadowing future difficulties for U.S. workers and world growth. Retail, accommodation and food service, and construction employment growth was largely supported by debt-financed consumption. The end of the housing bubble will likely limit future employment growth in those sectors as well. The retail sector is perhaps the only major non-tradeable sector that benefited from the internationalization of production; its cost reduction effects no doubt boosted sales, especially of consumer electronics and apparel.

As noted above, trends in employment creation in the tradeable sector have been dismal, strongly suggesting that workers have good reason to fear the ongoing restructuring of the U.S. economy in line with global accumulation dynamics. Growing numbers of workers will be forced to compete for jobs in the non-tradeable sector at a time when employment opportunities in that sector will likely also be limited.

Of course, the lack of aggregate job growth in the tradeable sector masks the existence of divergent trends within the sector. In particular, the internationalization of production did produce employment gains in industries that service transnational corporations and their international operations. As Spence and Hlatshwayo point out, "The tradable sector experienced job growth in high-end services including management and consulting services, computer systems design, finance, and insurance. These increases were roughly matched by declines in employment in most areas of manufacturing."[118]

Despite the boost to growth from the rapid run-up in consumer debt, private sector employment gains in the non-tradeable sector were not large enough to compensate for the lack of job creation in the tradeable sector. Michael Mandel sums up the situation as follows:

> Between May 1999 and May 2009, employment in the private sector only rose by 1.1 percent, by far the lowest 10-year increase in the post-Depression period. It's impossible to overstate how bad this is. Basically speaking, the private sector job machine has almost completely stalled over the past ten years.

> Over the past 10 years, the private sector has generated roughly 1.1 million additional jobs, or about 100K per year. The public sector created about 2.4 million jobs.

> But even that gives the private sector too much credit. Remember that the private sector includes health care, social assistance, and education, all areas which receive a lot of government support.

Without a decade of growing government support from rising health and education spending and soaring budget deficits, the labor market would have been flat on its back.[119]

Total private sector wage growth, critical to any sustainable consumption driven expansion, has also stagnated. As Jed Graham noted:

The increase in total real private-sector wages over the period 2001–11 was smaller than in any other 10-year period since World War II. In fact, its 4 percent growth rate was even lower than the 5 percent increase from 1929 to 1939. To put that in perspective, since the Great Depression, 10-year gains in real private wages had always exceeded 25 percent with one exception: the period ending in 1982–83, when the jobless rate spiked above 10 percent and wage gains briefly decelerated to 16 percent.[120]

Significantly, the lack of net job creation in the tradeable sector, especially in manufacturing, did not translate into a decline in value added. According to Spence and Hlatshwayo, "Value added in the tradable and non-tradable parts of the economy grew at similar rates [over the years 1990 to 2008]. In fact, the tradable sector, though smaller than the non-tradable, grew slightly faster and hence marginally increased its share of total value added, in marked contrast to the employment trends."[121]

Ironically, the cause of both the loss in employment and rise in value added in tradeable sectors like manufacturing was the same: the internationalization of production. The decline in manufacturing employment was largely caused by the rise in cross-border production activity. At the same time, by cheapening the cost of production, such activity not only expanded the market for many manufactures (such as consumer electronics), it also widened the gap between their final sales price and production cost, thereby raising both the profitability of and value added generated by many manufacturing firms. Apple products, discussed above, offer a useful example. Tradeable value added over the period 1990 to 2008 rose by 363 percent in electronics. By comparison it only rose by 72 percent in professional, scientific, and engineering services, and 56 percent in finance and insurance.[122]

This outcome makes clear why U.S. transnational corporations, especially those involved in the tradeable sector, have embraced the internationalization of production despite its domestic costs. Transnational manufacturers have directly profited from it. Transnational retailers have also benefited. Indeed, retailers like Walmart have aggressively pushed manufacturers to move their production offshore in order to lower production costs. Finally, the new international division of labor has also created profitable opportunities for business and financial service companies. This reality highlights the critical importance of studying capitalist dynamics from a class rather than nation-state perspective.

Stagnation Ahead

As we have seen, the economies of many countries, especially those in East Asia and the United States, have become intertwined in complex ways that have left them all increasingly unbalanced and unstable. While the U.S. economy has "officially" recovered from the Great Recession, employment and wage conditions remain depressed. As a result, consumer spending continues to be severely constrained and can be expected to remain so for many years to come. As Stephen S. Roach explained:

> The number is 0.2%. It is the average annualized growth of U.S. consumer spending over the past 14 quarters—calculated in inflation-adjusted terms from the first quarter of 2008 to the second quarter of 2011. Never before in the post–World War II era have American consumers been so weak for so long. This one number encapsulates much of what is wrong today in the United States—and in the global economy. . . .

The reasons behind this are not hard to fathom. By exploiting a record credit bubble to borrow against an unprecedented property bubble, American consumers spent well beyond their means for many years. When both bubbles burst, over-extended U.S. households had no choice but to cut back and rebuild their damaged balance sheets by paying down outsize debt burdens and rebuilding depleted savings.

Yet, on both counts, balance-sheet repair has only just begun. While household-sector debt was pruned to 115 percent of disposable personal income in early 2011 from the peak of 130 percent it hit in 2007, it remains well in excess of the 75 percent average of the 1970–2000 period. And, while the personal saving rate rose to 5 percent of disposable income in the first half of 2011 from the rock-bottom 1.2 percent low hit in mid-2005, this is far short of the nearly 8 percent norm that prevailed during the last 30 years of the twentieth century.

With retrenchment and balance-sheet repair only in its early stages, the zombie-like behavior of American consumers should persist.[123]

U.S. economic problems will not be solved by time alone. A meaningful recovery will require a major restructuring of the U.S. economy and, as the government's response to the Great Recession made clear, this is not on the political agenda. The government deliberately resisted taking any actions that would have promoted structural change, choosing instead to support renewal of existing patterns of economic activity. It supported bailouts for the financial sector and a limited fiscal stimulus composed mostly of tax breaks and temporary extensions of social programs. Though these efforts did contribute to ending the recession, they were not bold enough to meaningfully boost investment or employment, much less overcome long-term stagnationist tendencies.[124] As a consequence they have produced only a weak recovery.

But these policies did serve their purpose: they foreclosed more radical demands for change and protected existing corporate interests. For instance, although real wages fell by almost 2 percent in 2011, corporate profits hit a record high in the third quarter of the same year. *Bloomberg Businessweek* offered the following explanation for how corporations continue to enjoy profits in the face of declining wages:

> Companies are improving margins and generating profits as wage growth for the American worker lags behind the prices of goods and services. . . .
>
> "A lot of the outperformance of profits has been due to the fact that margins are expanding," said Michael Feroli, chief U.S. economist at JPMorgan Chase & Co. in New York. "Firms have been able to keep prices intact even though labor costs have been declining."
>
> While benefiting the bottom line for businesses, the decline in inflation-adjusted wages bodes ill for the sustainability of economic growth as consumers may eventually be forced to cut back, Feroli said. Businesses have also been slow to redeploy their profits into new hiring.
>
> "So far what you've had is the government has been able to step in and prop up household purchasing power by various cuts in payroll taxes, various increases in social benefits," said Feroli. "That has sort of kept the whole thing going, but you might worry with real wages being hit spending is going to decline."[125]

In other words, as far as major corporations are concerned there is little reason to demand a change in economic strategy. The dismal employment conditions enable them to suppress wages, while tax cuts and social spending ensure sufficient demand. Although this strategy has its own limits in growing concerns about rising national debt and deficit spending, for the time being it appears that business and political leaders are content to maintain the status quo.

This determination on the part of elites to "stay the course" despite the crisis is also visible in East Asia, and with similar consequences for working people. East Asia's export dependence means that the U.S. economic slowdown will eventually take its toll on East Asian growth and, by extension, growth in many Latin American and Sub-Saharan African countries as well. As Roach noted:

> As an export-led region, Asia remains heavily dependent on end-market demand from consumers in the developed world. The export share of developing Asia's 12 largest economies rose from 35 percent of pan-regional output in the late 1990s to 45 percent in early 2007. Little wonder that every economy in the region either fell into recession or experienced sharp slowdowns when global trade plunged in late 2008.[126]

Many analysts have suggested that there is a simple solution to East Asia's problems. The region's governments need only begin a long overdue economic transformation with the aim of establishing domestic rather than foreign needs as the engine of economic activity. This would involve, among other things, supporting household consumption by boosting wages and expanding the social safety net, as well as providing direct support to those (largely small and medium-size) firms oriented toward the domestic market.

Such policies are just as unacceptable to those in power in East Asia as suggestions of bank nationalizations, public works programs, aggressive industrial policy, and labor law reform are to those in power in the United States. China offers a good example of why this is so. Just as in the United States, top Chinese political and business leaders continue to enjoy record profits, so they have little reason to press for a change in economic policy regardless of the costs borne by workers and farmers. As *Bloomberg News* pointed out:

> The richest 70 members of China's legislature added more to their wealth last year than the combined net worth of all 535

members of the U.S. Congress, the president and his Cabinet, and the nine Supreme Court justices.

The net worth of the 70 richest delegates in China's National People's Congress, which opens its annual session on March 5, rose to 565.8 billion yuan ($89.8 billion) in 2011, a gain of $11.5 billion from 2010, according to figures from the Hurun Report, which tracks the country's wealthy. That compares to the $7.5 billion net worth of all 660 top officials in the three branches of the U.S. government. . . .

"It is extraordinary to see this degree of a marriage of wealth and politics," said Kenneth Liberthal, director of the John L. Thornton China Center at Washington's Brookings Institution. "It certainly lends vivid texture to the widespread complaints in China about an extreme inequality of wealth in the country now."[127]

The difficulty in changing economic strategy in China, just as in the United States, goes far beyond short-term financial considerations. The internationalization of production has produced significant structural changes in patterns and relations of economic activity that cannot easily be changed. In the words of the Asian Development Bank:

There is the issue of production specificity. PRC final-goods exports tend to be specific to foreign markets, and much of the PRC's physical and human infrastructure is linked to a manufacturing sector that is geared for exports rather than for domestic consumption. For many of the PRC's East Asian and Southeast Asian intermediate-goods suppliers, the problem may be worse, as the parts and components that they produce are not likely to have domestic uses, specific as these are to the regional production network.[128]

Thus, though theoretically possible, it is hard to imagine that East Asian political leaders would voluntarily undertake such an enormous transformation, especially since it would conflict with corporate interests, foreign and domestic (and in many cases their own as well). Not surprisingly, then, the actual response of the Chinese government, echoing that of the U.S. government, was to embrace policies designed to maintain the existing economic structure. As noted above, it launched a number of expensive, large-scale, capital intensive infrastructure projects and pushed state banks to aggressively make loans. While the investment spending helped maintain the country's rapid rate of growth, most of the projects were unneeded and created few jobs. The loans went largely to finance property speculation or the expansion of state industries already suffering from overcapacity. This response did little to raise wages, expand the social safety net, or support small and medium-size businesses producing for the domestic market. It did, however, ensure continuing profits for those in power.

However, as previously discussed, Chinese policy initiatives are marked by contradictions that make them unsustainable.[129] As economist Noriel Roubini wrote:

The problem, of course, is that no country can be productive enough to reinvest 50% of GDP in new capital stock without eventually facing immense overcapacity and a staggering non-performing loan problem. China is rife with overinvestment in physical capital, infrastructure, and property. To a visitor, this is evident in sleek but empty airports and bullet trains (which will reduce the need for the 45 planned airports), highways to nowhere, thousands of colossal new central and provincial government buildings, ghost towns, and brand-new aluminum smelters kept closed to prevent global prices from plunging.

Commercial and high-end residential investment has been excessive, automobile capacity has outstripped even the recent surge in sales, and overcapacity in steel, cement, and other manufacturing sectors is increasing further. . . . Overcapacity will lead inevitably to serious deflationary pressures, starting with the manufacturing and real-estate sectors.[130]

It is of course difficult to predict the course of capitalist globalization with complete certainty.[131] At the same time, existing patterns of economic activity and class interests strongly suggest that world growth rates will continue to decline and economic conditions for the great majority of working people will continue to deteriorate regardless of country. The possibility of another worldwide crisis must also be taken seriously. The exploding debt and growth problems in Europe could well be the trigger. As Roach wrote, "With fiscal austerity likely to restrain aggregate demand in the years ahead, and with capital-short banks likely to curtail lending . . . a pan-European recession seems inevitable. . . . It is difficult to see how Asia can remain an oasis of prosperity in such a tough global climate. Yet denial is deep, and momentum is seductive."[132]

The political consequences of growing immiseration remain to be determined. To the extent that workers still think largely in national terms, they are vulnerable to state-corporate initiatives designed to encourage them to blame workers in other countries for their problems. On the other hand, the realities of contemporary capitalist accumulation dynamics, with workers everywhere suffering from similar competitiveness pressures, could create the basis for meaningful worker solidarity by promoting recognition that it is capitalism itself that is the cause of worsening social and economic conditions.

There are hopeful signs that workers are coming to realize that they must become proactive if they are to improve their living conditions. For example, growing numbers of Chinese workers have begun to aggressively defend their immediate interests, engaging in a number of coordinated workplace actions.[133] A *China Labor Bulletin* report on the Chinese workers' movement concluded that "workers are becoming more proactive," "their ability to organize is improving," and their "protests are becoming more successful."[134] There is also growing awareness among Chinese workers and farmers that the contemporary Chinese experience has little to do with socialism and growing interest in critically reengaging with China's past attempts to build it.[135] In the United States, struggles led by public sector workers and activists in the Occupy movement appear to have renewed popular support for direct action and interest in alternative economic and social visions.[136]

If working people are to escape the dire future that confronts them, these and other national struggles must grow into movements that aim at dramatically expanding the capacity and willingness of their respective national governments to regulate and redirect economic activity, which at a minimum means reversing past initiatives that encouraged the internationalization of production. Meaningful change will also require new thinking about strategies for economic renewal, including ways to build upon, while also transforming, the regional relationships created by capitalist globalization.

Unfortunately, despite the promise of renewed activism, the political impetus still remains in the hands of transnational capital. Looking to the future, we must ensure that history keeps a fine accounting of the consequences of their actions.

PART II

THE NEOLIBERAL PROJECT
AND RESISTANCE

2—Neoliberalism: Myths and Reality

Agreements like the North American Free Trade Agreement (NAFTA) and institutions like the World Trade Organization (WTO) have enhanced transnational capitalist power and profits at the cost of increasing economic instability and deteriorating working and living conditions. Despite this reality, neoliberal claims that liberalization, deregulation, and privatization produce unrivaled benefits are repeated so often that many working people accept them as unchallengeable truths. Thus business and political leaders in the United States and other developed capitalist countries routinely defend their efforts to expand the WTO and secure new agreements like the Free Trade Area of the Americas (FTAA) as necessary to ensure a brighter future for the world's people, especially those living in poverty.

For example, Renato Ruggiero, the first Director-General of the WTO, declared that WTO liberalization efforts have "the potential for eradicating global poverty in the early part of the next [twenty-first] century—a utopian notion even a few decades ago, but a real possibility today."[1] Similarly, writing shortly before the December 2005 WTO ministerial meeting in Hong Kong, William Cline, a senior fellow for the Institute for International Economics, claimed that "if all global trade barriers were eliminated, approximately 500 million people could be lifted out of poverty over 15 years. . . . The current Doha Round of multilateral trade negotiations in the World Trade Organization provides the best single chance for the international community to achieve these gains."[2]

Therefore, if we are going to mount an effective challenge to the neoliberal globalization project, we must redouble our efforts to win the "battle of ideas." Winning this battle requires, among other things, demonstrating that neoliberalism functions as an ideological cover for the promotion of capitalist interests, not as a scientific framework for illuminating the economic and social consequences of capitalist dynamics. It also requires showing the processes by which capitalism, as an international system, undermines rather than promotes working-class interests in both third world and developed capitalist countries.

The Myth of the Superiority of "Free Trade": Theoretical Arguments

According to supporters of the WTO and the FTAA, both seek to promote free trade in order to enhance efficiency and maximize economic well-being.[3] This focus on trade hides what is in fact a much broader political-economic agenda: the expansion and enhancement of corporate profit-making opportunities. In the case of the WTO, this agenda has been pursued through a variety of agreements that are explicitly designed to limit or block public regulation of economic activity in contexts that have little to do with trade as normally understood.[4]

For example, the Agreement on Trade-Related Aspects of Intellectual Property Rights (TRIPS) limits the ability of states to deny patents on certain products (including living organisms) or control the use of products patented in their respective nations (including the use of compulsory licensing to ensure affordability of critical medicines). It also forces states to accept a significant increase in the length of time during which patents remain in force. The Agreement on Trade-Related Investment Measures (TRIMS) restricts the ability of states to put performance requirements on foreign direct investment (FDI), encompassing those that would require the use of local inputs (including labor) or technology transfer. A proposed expansion of the General Agreement on Trade in Services (GATS) would force states to open their national service markets (which include everything from health care and education to public utilities and retail trade) to foreign providers as well as limit public regulation of their activity. Similarly, a proposed Government Procurement Agreement would deny states the ability to use non-economic criteria, such as labor and environmental practices, in awarding contracts.

These agreements are rarely discussed in the mainstream media precisely because they directly raise issues of private versus public power and are not easily defended. This is one of the most important reasons why those who support the capitalist globalization project prefer to describe the institutional arrangements that help underpin it as trade agreements and defend them on the basis of the alleged virtues of free trade. This is a defense that unfortunately and undeservedly holds enormous sway among working people, especially in the developed capitalist countries. And, using free trade as a theoretical foundation, capitalist globalization advocates find it relatively easy to encourage popular acceptance of the broader proposition that market-determined outcomes are superior to socially determined ones in all spheres of activity. Therefore, it is critical that we develop an effective and accessible critique of this myth of the superiority of free trade. In fact, this is an easier task than is generally assumed.

Arguments promoting free trade generally rest on the theory of comparative advantage. David Ricardo introduced this theory in 1821 in his *Principles of Political Economy and Taxation*. It is commonly misunderstood, to assert the obvious, that countries have or can create different comparative advantages or that trade can be helpful. In fact, this theory supports a very specific policy conclusion: a country's best economic policy is to allow unregulated international market activity to determine its comparative advantage and national patterns of production.[5]

Ricardo "proved" his theory of comparative advantage using a two-country, static model of the world in which Portugal is assumed to be a more efficient producer of both wine and cloth than England, but with greatest superiority in wine production. Ricardo demonstrated that, in his created world, both Portugal and England would gain by an international division of labor in which each produced the good in which it had the greatest relative or comparative advantage. Thus, even though England's production efficiency was inferior to that of Portugal in both goods, the logic of free trade would lead Portugal to concentrate on wine production and England on cloth production, with the resulting trade between them generating maximum benefits for both countries.

Mainstream economists, while continuing to accept the basic outlines of Ricardo's theory, have developed refinements to it. The most important are the Hecksher-Olin theory, which argues that since a country's comparative advantage is shaped by its resource base, capital-poor third world countries should specialize in labor-intensive products; the factor-price equalization theory, which argues that free trade will raise the price of the intensively used factor (which will be unskilled labor in the third world) until all factor prices are equalized worldwide; and the Stopler-Samuelson theory, which argues that the incomes of the scarce factor (labor in rich countries, capital in poor countries) will suffer the most from free trade. None of these refinements challenges the basic conclusion of Ricardo's theory of comparative advantage. Rather, they offer additional support for the argument that workers in the third world will be the greatest beneficiaries of free trade.

Like all theories, the theory of comparative advantage (and its conclusion) is based on a number of assumptions. Among the most important are:

- Perfect competition exists between firms.
- Full employment of all factors of production.
- Labor and capital are perfectly mobile within a country and do not move across national borders.
- A country's gains from trade are captured by those living in the country and spent locally.
- A country's external trade is always in balance.
- Market prices accurately reflect the real (or social) costs of the products produced.

Even a quick consideration of these assumptions reveals that they are extensive and unrealistic. Moreover, if they are not satisfied, there is no basis for accepting the theory's conclusion that free-market policies will promote international well-being. For example, the assumption of full employment of all factors of production, including labor, is obviously false. Equally problematic is the theory's implied restructuring process, which assumes that (but never explains how) workers who lose their jobs as a result of free trade–generated imports will quickly find new employment in the expanding export sector of the economy. In reality, workers (and other factors of production) may not be equally productive in alternative uses. Even if we ignore this problem, if their reallocation is not sufficiently fast, the newly liberalized economy will likely suffer an increase in unemployment, leading to a reduction in aggregate demand and perhaps recession. Thus, even if all factors of production eventually become fully employed, it is quite possible that the cost of adjustment would outweigh the alleged efficiency gains from the trade-induced restructuring.

The assumption that prices reflect social costs is also problematic. Many product markets are dominated by monopolies; many firms receive substantial government subsidies that influence their production and pricing decisions; and many production activities generate significant negative externalities (especially environmental ones). Therefore trade specialization based on existing market prices could easily produce a structure of international economic activity with lower overall efficiency, leading to a reduction in social well-being.

There is also reason to challenge the assumption that external trade will remain in balance. This assumption depends on another assumption—that exchange rate movements will automatically and quickly correct trade imbalances. However, exchange rates can easily be influenced by speculative financial activity, causing them to move in destabilizing rather than equilibrating directions. In addition, with foreign trade increasingly shaped by the logic of transnational corporate controlled cross-border production networks, it is far less likely that exchange rate movements will generate the desired new patterns of production and trade. To the extent that exchange rate movements fail to produce the necessary trade adjustments in a reasonably short period, imports will have to be reduced (and the trade balance restored) through a forced reduction in aggregate demand, and perhaps recession.

Also worthy of challenge is the assumption that capital is not highly mobile across national borders. This assumption helps to underpin others, including the assumptions of full employment and balanced trade. If capital is highly mobile, then free market/ free trade policies could produce capital flight leading to dein-dustrialization, unbalanced trade, unemployment, and economic crisis. In short, the free trade–supporting policy recommenda-tions that flow from the theory of comparative advantage rest on a series of very dubious assumptions.[6]

The Myth of the Superiority of "Free Trade": Empirical Arguments

Proponents of neoliberal policies often cite the results of highly sophisticated simulation studies to buttress their arguments. But these studies are seriously flawed, in large part because they rely on many of the same assumptions as the theory of comparative advantage. The following examination of two prominent studies reveals how reliance on these assumptions undermines the credibility of their results.

In 2001, Drusilla Brown, Alan Deardoff, and Robert Stern published a study that claimed that a WTO-sponsored elimination of all trade barriers would add $1.9 trillion to the world's gross economic product by 2005.[7] Their study was widely showcased in media stories that appeared before the November 2001 start of WTO negotiations in Doha, Qatar.

The World Bank has also attempted to calculate, as part of its Global Economic Prospects series, the expected benefits from trade liberalization. In *Global Economic Prospects 2002*, it concluded that "faster integration through lowering barriers to merchandise trade would increase growth and provide some $1.5 trillion of additional cumulative income to developing countries over the period 2005–2015. Liberalization of services in developing countries could provide even greater gains—perhaps as much as four times larger than this amount. [The results also] show that labor's share of national income would rise throughout the developing world."[8]

The studies by Brown, Deardoff, and Stern, and the World Bank are based on computable general equilibrium models, in which economies are defined by a set of interconnected markets. When prices change—in this case because of a change in tariffs—national product markets are assumed to adjust to restore equilibrium. Since economies are themselves connected through trade, price changes are also assumed to generate more complex global adjustments before a new equilibrium outcome is achieved. It is on the basis of such modeling that the authors of these studies try to determine the economic consequences of trade liberalization.

This type of modeling is very challenging. Specific assumptions must be made about consumer and producer behavior in different markets and in different nations, including their speed of adjustment. Detailed national input-output tables are also required. But even more is needed. For example, in order to ensure that their model will be solvable, Brown, Deardoff, and Stern assume that there is only one unique equilibrium outcome for each trade liberalization scenario. They also assume there are just two inputs, capital and labor, which are perfectly mobile across sectors in each country but bound by national borders. In addition, they assume total aggregate expenditure in each economy is sufficient and will automatically adjust to ensure full employment of all resources. Finally, they also assume that flexible exchange rates will prevent tariff changes from causing changes in trade balances.

Said differently, the authors created a model in which liberalization cannot, by assumption, cause or worsen unemployment, capital flight, or trade imbalances. Thanks to these assumptions, if a country drops its trade restrictions, market forces will quickly and effortlessly encourage capital and labor to shift into new, more productive uses. And, since trade always remains in balance, this restructuring will, by definition, generate a dollar's worth of new exports for every dollar's worth of new imports. As Peter Dorman notes in his critique of this study: "Of course, workers and governments would have little to worry about in such a world—provided they could shift readily between expanding and contracting sectors of the economy."[9]

World Bank economists also use computable general equilibrium modeling in their work. In *Global Economic Prospects 2002*, they begin their simulation study with "a baseline view about the likely evolution of developing countries, based upon best guesses about generally stable parameters—savings, investment, population growth, trade and productivity growth."[10] This baseline view incorporates only those changes in the "global trading regime" that occurred up through 1997 and uses these best guesses to estimate economic outcomes for the years 2005 to 2015. Next they assume the removal of all trade restrictions in the period 2005 to 2010, with the restrictions reduced by one-sixth in each year.[11] Finally, they compare the estimated economic outcomes from this liberalization scenario with those from the initial baseline scenario to determine the gains from liberalization.

This modeling effort also depends on several critical and unrealistic assumptions. One is that tariff reductions will have no effect on government deficits—they will remain unchanged from what they were in the baseline projection. This assumption claims that governments will automatically be able to replace lost tariff revenue with new revenue from other sources. Another assumption is that tariff reductions will have no effect on trade balances; they will remain the same as in the baseline projection. The final one is the existence of full employment. Once again, a powerful free-trade bias is built into the heart of the model by assumption, thereby ensuring a pro-liberalization outcome.

Although this bias is sufficient to dismiss the study's usefulness as a guide to policy, its results are still worth examining, for two reasons. First, the projected benefits are smaller than one might imagine given the World Bank's unqualified support for liberalization. Second, later World Bank studies have revealed significantly smaller benefits. In its 2002 study, the World Bank concluded that "measured in static terms, world income in 2015 would be $355 billion more with [merchandise] trade liberalization than in the baseline."[12] Third world countries as a group would receive $184 billion, or approximately 52 percent of these total benefits. Significantly, $142 billion of this third world gain is projected to come from the liberalization of trade in agricultural goods. Even more noteworthy, $114 billion is estimated to come from third world liberalization of its own agricultural sector.[13] Liberalization of trade in manufactures turns out to be a minor affair. Total estimated third world gains from a complete liberalization of world trade in manufactures amount to only $44 billion.

If we were to take these numbers seriously, they certainly suggest that the third world has little to gain from an actual WTO agreement. As Mark Weisbrot and Dean Baker note in their critique of this study, "The removal of all of the rich countries' barriers to the merchandise exports of developing countries—including agriculture, textiles, and other manufactured goods—would...when such changes were fully implemented by 2015 ... add 0.6 percent to the GDP of low- and middle-income countries. This means that a country in Sub-Saharan Africa that would, under present trade arrangements, have a per capita income of $500 per year in 2015, would instead have a per capita income of $503."[14] Moreover, as also pointed out, these meager gains would be far outweighed by losses incurred from compliance with other associated WTO agreements.

More recent World Bank estimates show even smaller gains from liberalization. In *Global Economic Prospects 2005*, the World Bank incorporated new data sets, which allowed it to "capture the considerable reform between 1997 and 2001 (e.g., continued implementation of the Uruguay Round and China's progress toward WTO accession), and an improved treatment of preferential trade agreements."[15] As a result, total projected static gains from merchandise trade liberalization fell to $260 billion (in 2015 relative to the baseline scenario), with only 41 percent of the gains accruing to the third world.[16]

Although working people have been ill-served by capitalist globalization, many are reluctant to challenge it because they have been intimidated by the "scholarly" arguments of those who support it. However, as we have seen, these arguments are based on theories and highly artificial simulations that deliberately misrepresent the workings of capitalism. They can and should be challenged and rejected.

Neoliberalism: The Reality

The post-1980 neoliberal era has been marked by slower growth, greater trade imbalances, and deteriorating social conditions. The United Nations Conference on Trade and Development (UNCTAD) reports: "For developing countries as a whole (excluding China), the average trade deficit in the 1990s is higher than in the 1970s by almost 3 percentage points of GDP, while the average growth rate is lower by 2 percent per annum."[17] Moreover,

> the pattern is broadly similar in all developing regions. In Latin America the average growth rate is lower by 3 percent

per annum in the 1990s than in the 1970s, while trade deficits as a proportion of GDP are much the same. In Sub-Saharan Africa growth fell, but deficits rose. The Asian countries managed to grow faster in the 1980s, while reducing their payments deficits, but in the 1990s they have run greater deficits without achieving faster growth.[18]

A study by Mark Weisbrot, Dean Baker, and David Rosnick on the consequences of neoliberal policies on third world development comes to similar conclusions. The authors note that "contrary to popular belief, the past 25 years (1980–2005) have seen a sharply slower rate of economic growth and reduced progress on social indicators for the vast majority of low- and middle-income countries [compared with the prior two decades]."[19]

For those that reject the major assumptions underlying mainstream arguments for the "freeing" of international economic activity, this outcome is not surprising. Trade liberalization contributed to the deindustrialization of many third world countries, thereby increasing their import dependence. By making them cheaper and easier to obtain, it also encouraged an increase in the importation of luxury goods. And finally, by attracting transnational corporate production to the third world, it also increased the import intensity of most third world exports. Export earnings could not keep pace, largely because growing third world export activity and competition (prompted by the need to offset the rise in imports) tended to drive down export earnings. Exports were also limited by slower growth and protectionism in most developed capitalist countries.

In an effort to keep growing trade and current account deficits manageable, third world states, often pressured by the IMF and World Bank, used austerity measures (especially draconian cuts in social programs) to slow economic growth (and imports). They also deregulated capital markets, privatized economic activity, and relaxed regulation of foreign investment in an effort to attract the financing needed to offset the existing deficits. While devastating to working people and national development possibilities, these policies were, as intended, responsive to the interests of transnational capital and a small but influential sector of third world capital. This is the reality of neoliberalism.

The Dynamics of Contemporary Capitalism

Though the term *neoliberalism* does, in many ways, capture the essence of contemporary capitalist practices and policies, it is also in some important respects a problematic term. In particular, it encourages the view that a wide range of policy options simultaneously exist under capitalism, with neoliberalism just one of the possibilities. States could reject neoliberalism, if they wanted, and implement more social democratic or interventionist policies, similar to those employed in the 1960s and 1970s. Unfortunately, things are not so simple. The "freeing" of economic activity that is generally identified with neoliberalism is not so much a bad policy choice as it is a forced structural response on the part of many third world states to capitalist-generated tensions and contradictions. Said differently, it is capitalism (as a dynamic and exploitative system) rather than neoliberalism (as a set of policies) that must be challenged and overcome.

Mainstream theorists usually consider international trade, finance, and investment as separate processes. But the fact is they are interrelated. And, as highlighted above, the capitalist drive for greater profitability has generally worked to pressure third world states into an overarching liberalization and deregulation. This dynamic has had important consequences, especially, but not exclusively, for the third world. In particular, it has encouraged transnational corporations to advance their aims through the establishment and extension of international production networks. This has led to new forms of dominance over third world industrial activity that involve its reshaping and integration across borders in ways that are ever more destructive to the social, economic, and political needs of working people.

During the 1960s and 1970s, most third world countries pursued state-directed import-substitution industrialization strategies and financed their trade deficits with bank loans. This pattern ended suddenly in the early 1980s, when economic instabilities in the developed capitalist world, especially in the United States, led to rising interest rates and global recession. Third world borrowing costs soared and export earnings plummeted, triggering the third world "debt crisis." With debt repayment in question, banks greatly reduced their lending, leading to ever deepening third world economic and social problems.

To overcome these problems, third world states sought new ways to boost exports and new sources of international funds. Increasingly, they came to see export-oriented foreign direct investment as the answer. The competition for this investment was fierce. Country after country made changes in their investment regimes, with the great majority designed to create a more liberalized, deregulated, and "business friendly" environment. Transnational corporations responded eagerly to these changes, many of which they and their governments helped promote. And, from 1991 to 1998, foreign direct investment became the single greatest source of net capital inflow into the third world, accounting for 34 percent of the total.[20]

New technologies had made it possible for transnational corporations to cheapen production costs for many goods by segmenting and geographically dividing their production processes. They thus used their investments to locate the labor-intensive production segments of these goods—in particular the production or assembly of parts and components—in the third world. This was especially true for electronic and electrical goods, clothing and apparel, and certain technologically advanced goods such as optical instruments.

The result was the establishment or expansion of numerous vertically structured international production networks, many of which extended over several different countries. According to UNCTAD, "It has been estimated, on the basis of input-output tables from a number of OECD and emerging-market countries, that trade based on specialization within vertical production networks accounts for up to 30 percent of world exports, and that it has grown by as much as 40 percent in the last 25 years."[21]

Despite the fierce third world competition to attract FDI, transnational corporations tended to concentrate their investments in only a few countries. In general, U.S. capital emphasized North America (NAFTA), Japanese capital focused on East Asia, and European capital on Central Europe. The countries that "lost out" in the FDI competition were generally forced to manage their trade and finance problems with austerity. Those countries that "won" usually experienced a relatively fast industrial transformation. More specifically, they became major exporters of manufactures, especially high-technology products such as transistors and semiconductors, computers, parts of computers and office machines, telecommunications equipment and parts, and electrical machinery.

As a consequence of this development, the share of third world exports that were manufactures soared from 20 percent in the 1970s and early 1980s, to 70 percent by the late 1990s.[22] The third world share of world manufacturing exports also jumped from 4.4 percent in 1965 to 30.1 percent in 2003.[23]

Mainstream economists claim that this rise in manufactured exports demonstrates the benefits of liberalization, and thus the importance of WTO-style liberalization agreements for development. However, this argument falsely identifies FDI and exports of manufactures with development, thereby seriously misrepresenting the dynamics of transnational capital accumulation. The reality is that participation in transnational corporate-controlled production networks has done little to support rising standards of living, economic stability, or national development prospects.

There are many reasons for this failure. First, those countries that have succeeded in attracting FDI have usually done so in the context of liberalizing and deregulating their economies. This has generally resulted in the destruction of their domestic import-competing industries, causing unemployment, a rapid rise in imports, and industrial hollowing out. Second, the activities located in the third world rarely transfer skills or technology, or encourage domestic industrial linkages. This means that these activities are seldom able to promote a dynamic or nationally integrated process of development. Furthermore, the exports produced are highly import-dependent, thereby greatly reducing their foreign exchange earning benefits.

Finally, the transnational accumulation process makes third world growth increasingly dependent on external demand. In most cases, the primary final market for these networks is the United States, which means that third world growth comes to depend ever more on the ability of the United States to sustain ever larger trade deficits—an increasingly dubious proposition.

Few countries have escaped these problems. For example, UNCTAD studied the economic performances of "seven of the more advanced developing countries" over the period 1981 to 1996: Hong Kong, Malaysia, Mexico, Republic of Korea, Singapore, Taiwan, and Turkey. These are among the most successful exporters of manufactures. Yet, because much of their export activity is organized within transnational corporate-controlled production networks, the gains to worker well-being or national development have been limited.

For example, average manufacturing value added for the group as a whole remained consistently below the value of manufactured exports over the entire period, with the ratio declining from 76 percent in 1981 to 55 percent in 1996. And, though the group's average ratio of manufactured exports to GDP rose sharply, its average ratio of manufacturing value added to GDP generally remained unchanged.[24] Moreover, though the group as a whole maintained a rough balance in manufactured goods trade until the late 1980s, after that point imports grew much faster than exports. Mexico's experience perhaps best symbolizes the bankruptcy of this growth strategy: "Between 1980 and 1997 Mexico's share in world manufactured exports rose tenfold, while its share in world manufacturing value added fell by more than one-third, and its share in world income (at current dollars) [fell] by about 13 percent."[25]

China: The Latest Neoliberal Success Story

Capitalism's failure to deliver development is not due to its lack of dynamism; indeed, quite the opposite is true. By intensifying the development and application of new production and exchange relationships within and between countries, this dynamism causes rapid shifts in the economic fortunes of nations, creating a constantly changing (and shrinking) group of "winners" and (an ever larger) group of "losers," and masking the connection between the two. Even East Asia has been subject to the instabilities of capitalist dynamics: the East Asian crisis of 1997–98 devastated such past "star performers" as South Korea, Indonesia, Thailand, and Malaysia. After quickly distancing themselves from these countries (and their past praise for their growth), most neoliberals have now eagerly embraced a new champion, China.[26]

According to the conventional wisdom, China has become the third world's biggest recipient of foreign direct investment, the leading exporter of manufactures, and has the fastest-growing economy, largely because its government adopted a growth strategy based on privileging private enterprise and international market forces. In response to this new strategy, net FDI in China grew from $3.5 billion in 1990 to $60.6 billion in 2004. Foreign manufacturing affiliates now account for approximately one-third of China's total manufacturing sales. They also produce 55 percent of the country's exports and a significantly greater percentage of its higher technology exports. As a consequence of these trends, the country's ratio of exports to GDP has climbed steadily, from 16 percent in 1990 to 36 percent in 2003.[27] Thus China's growth has become increasingly dependent on export activity organized by transnational corporations.

Foreign investment has indeed transformed China into a fast-growing export platform, with some significant domestic production capacity. At the same time, many of the limitations of this growth strategy are also visible in China. For example, foreign-dominated export activity has done little to support the development of nationally integrated production or technology supply networks. Moreover, as the Chinese state continues to lose its planning and directing capability, and the country's resources are increasingly incorporated into foreign networks largely for the purpose of satisfying external market demands, the country's autonomous development potential is being lost.

China's growth has enriched a relatively small but numerically significant upper-income group of Chinese, who enjoy greatly expanded consumption opportunities. However, these gains have been largely underwritten by the exploitation of the great majority of Chinese working people. For example, as a consequence of Chinese state liberalization policies, state-owned enterprises laid off 30 million workers over the period 1998 to 2004. With urban unemployment rates in double digits, few of these former state workers were able to find adequate reemployment. As a result, over 21.8 million of them depend on the government's "average minimum living allowance" for their survival. As of June 2005, this allowance was equal to approximately $19 a month; by comparison, the average monthly income of an urban worker was approximately $165.[28]

Though the new foreign-dominated export production has generated new employment opportunities, most of these jobs are extremely low paid. A consultant for the U.S. Bureau of Labor Statistics has estimated that Chinese factory workers earn an average of 64 cents an hour (including benefits).[29] In Guangdong, where approximately a third of China's exports are produced, base manufacturing wages have been frozen for the past decade. Moreover, few if any of these workers have access to affordable housing, health care, pensions, or education.[30]

China's economic transformation has come not only at high cost for Chinese working people, it has also intensified (and benefited from) the contradictions of capitalist development in other countries, including in East Asia. For example, China's export successes in advanced capitalist markets, in particular that of the United States, have forced other East Asian producers out of those markets. Out of necessity, they have reoriented their export activity to the production of parts and components for use by export-oriented transnational corporations operating in China. Thus all of East Asia is being knitted together into a regional accumulation regime that crosses many borders and in so doing restructures national activity and resources away from meeting domestic needs. Activity and resources are instead being organized to serve export markets out of the region under the direction of transnational corporations whose interests are largely in cost reduction regardless of the social or environmental consequences.[31]

The much slower post-crisis growth of East Asian countries and the heightened competitiveness pressures that are squeezing living standards throughout the region provide strong proof that this new arrangement of regional economic relations is incapable of promoting a stable process of long-term development. Meanwhile, China's export explosion has also accelerated the industrial hollowing out of the Japanese and U.S. economies, as well as the unsustainable U.S. trade deficit.

At some point the (economic and political) imbalances generated by this accumulation process will become too great, and corrections will have to take place. Insofar as the logic of capitalist competition goes unchallenged, governments can be expected to manage the adjustment process with policies that will likely worsen conditions for workers in both third world and developed capitalist countries. Neoliberal advocates can also be expected to embrace this process of adjustment as the means to "discover" their next success story, whose experience will then be cited as proof of the superiority of market forces.

Our Challenge

As we have seen, arguments purporting to demonstrate that free trade/free market policies will transform economic activities and relations in ways that universally benefit working people are based on theories and simulations that distort the actual workings of capitalism. The reality is that growing numbers of workers are being captured by an increasingly unified and transnational process of capital accumulation. Wealth is being generated, but working people in all the countries involved are being pitted against one another and suffering similar consequences, including unemployment and worsening living and working conditions.

Working people and their communities are engaged in growing, although uneven, resistance to the situation. While increasingly effective, this resistance still remains largely defensive and politically unfocused. One reason is that neoliberal theory continues to provide a powerful ideological cover for capitalist globalization, despite the fact that it is generated by and designed to advance capitalist class interests. Another is the dynamic nature of contemporary capitalism, which tends to mask its destructive nature. Therefore, as participants in the resistance, we must work to ensure that our many struggles are waged in ways that help working people better understand the nature of the accumulation processes that are reshaping our lives. In this way, we can illuminate the common capitalist roots of the problems we face and the importance of building movements committed to radical social transformation and (international) solidarity.

3—Capitalism, the Korea-U.S. Free Trade Agreement, and Resistance

In 2011, the Obama administration overcame the opposition of many U.S. activists to win congressional approval of free trade agreements (FTAs) with South Korea, Colombia, and Panama, and U.S. activists are working hard in opposition.[1] FTAs play a very important role in contemporary capitalism, promoting and securing the operation of transnational production networks. Because they establish and reinforce patterns of economic activity that are destructive of majority interests, they should be opposed. At issue is how best to oppose them.

The goal of this chapter is to contribute to the development of an effective U.S. strategy to defeat FTAs. It first considers the evolving role of FTAs in supporting contemporary capitalist accumulation dynamics. Then, it scrutinizes the Korea-U.S. FTA (KORUS FTA), examining the motivations that led to its negotiation, the content of the agreement, and the arguments U.S. government officials and institutions made in support of its ratification. The chapter concludes with a critical evaluation of the efforts by U.S. and Korean opponents of its ratification and a call for a new organizing strategy.

Capitalist Accumulation Dynamics

One cannot appreciate the significance of FTAs divorced from a consideration of the dynamics of capitalist accumulation. A new phase in the organization of production, marked by a change in the internationalization of U.S. manufacturing activity, began in the late 1960s–early 1970s. U.S. transnational corporations had been active in the third world before this period, but their activity at that time was primarily to access third world markets protected by tariffs. This new phase involved the establishment of third world export platforms to cheapen the cost of producing goods for sale throughout the world, including the home market.

U.S. corporations were the first movers, but transnational corporations from other countries soon adopted the same cost-cutting strategy. In 1971, U.S. transnational corporations had 1,337 foreign affiliates, while Japanese and German transnational corporations had only 13 and 80, respectively. The totals for 1983 were 1,339, 64, and 241. The totals for 1998 were 2,901, 2,296, and 1,764.[2]

Initially, this internationalization of production was primarily limited to garments and simple consumer electronics. By the 1990s, however, it had expanded to include more technologically sophisticated manufactures, such as automobiles, televisions, computers, power and machine tools, cameras, cell phones, pharmaceuticals, and semiconductors.

Equally significant, this product expansion was associated with another restructuring of transnational corporate activity. Corporations began dividing the production process into ever finer segments, both vertical and horizontal, and locating the separate stages in two or more countries, creating cross-border production networks. As Prema-Chandra Athukorala and Jayant Menon noted, "Over the years, production networks have evolved to encompass multiple countries in different stages of the assembly process. Today, product fragments will typically have gone through multiple border crossings before being incorporated into a final product."[3]

Though these production networks remain dominated by core-country transnational corporations, many of these now rely on independent contract manufacturers to procure the necessary parts and components and oversee their assembly into final products.[4] Often these independent contract manufacturers have themselves become transnational in their operation. As a consequence, many core-country transnational corporations are no longer directly involved in production. Rather, they maintain their dominance through their control over product design and marketing.

The complex nature of this strategy, which involves a variety of business relationships, means that trends in the international trade of components are a better measure of the importance of cross-border production networks than are changes in foreign direct investment. Not surprisingly, international trade statistics provide confirmation of the growing centrality of cross-border production activity.[5] They also highlight East Asia's leading position in international manufacturing production.

The trade in components grew from 18.9 percent of total exports of manufacturers in 1992–93 to 22.3 percent in 2005–6, accounting for approximately one-fourth of the total increase in world manufacturing exports. Over this same period, the third world share of component trade grew from 27 percent to 47 percent. Although a global phenomenon, developing East Asia dominates this trade. Its share of world component trade grew from 17.8 percent in 1992–93 to 32.3 percent in 2005–6. In 2005–06, it accounted for more than two-thirds of the total component trade of third world countries.[6]

A more detailed examination of trade patterns reveals the link between transnational capital's cross-border production strategy and the explosion in East Asian trade in components. The most common goods produced using this strategy are high-value-added products involving significant labor intensive operations, especially information and communication technology (ICT) products (such as computers and telecom equipment) and electrical goods (such as semiconductors and semiconductor devices).

In line with this strategy, "Semiconductors and other electronics components alone accounted for 50 percent of component exports from East Asia in 2004–5. Adding components of telecommunication equipment and office and automated data processing machines to these items increases the concentration ratio to almost 90 percent of total exports of components."[7] In addition, these components are largely being traded from one East Asian country to another. "The intraregional share of developing Asia's parts and component trade rose by almost 20 percentage points over the past decade, reaching 62 percent in 2005–2006, as compared to an 8 percentage point increase in total trade in manufacturing over the same period."[8]

As the Asian Development Bank makes clear, the People's Republic of China (PRC) has come to play the central role in transnational capital's regional strategy:

> There is the cluster of highly interdependent, open, and vibrant economies in East Asia and Southeast Asia that include the NIEs [Newly Industrialized Economies], the PRC, and the more advanced countries of ASEAN [Association of Southeast Asian Nations]. With the PRC at the center of the assembly process and with exports going mainly to the United States and Europe, production in and trade among these economies have been increasingly organized through vertical specialization in networks, with intense trade in parts and components, particularly in the ICT and electrical machinery industries.[9]

China's unique position as the region's production platform for the export of final goods is highlighted by the fact that it is the only country in the region that runs a deficit in components trade, and whose exports are overwhelmingly final products. This unique position has enabled China to increase its share of world exports of ICT products from 3 percent in 1992 to 24 percent in 2006, and its share of electrical goods from 4 percent to 21 percent over the same period.[10] Of course, most of these are not truly Chinese exports, but rather exports assembled or produced in China;

foreign corporations are responsible for approximately 88 percent of all Chinese high-technology exports.[11]

In short, East Asia has become the center of transnational capital's restructuring activity and capitalist accumulation and growth. At the same time, transnational corporations have also established similar production networks in Latin America and the Caribbean, as well as in Europe. And, although I have emphasized production dynamics, these are intimately tied to non-manufacturing activities. For example, many transnational retailers derive substantial profits from selling the goods produced by these networks. Similarly, many transnational financial service firms benefit from financing the relevant manufacturing activity and associated currency flows and trade imbalances. In sum, although capitalist accumulation dynamics are not reducible to the transnational activity discussed above, this activity has become central to the profit-making activities of many of the world's most powerful capitalist enterprises.

The Significance of FTAs

The growth of cross-border production networks has been supported by new technological innovations in communications and transportation as well as policy initiatives designed to promote trade and investment. FTAs are one of the most important policy initiatives, ensuring that transnational corporations will be able to:

- import and export goods free from tariffs and non-tariff barriers.
- move funds across borders free from capital controls and other financial restrictions.
- invest without fear of performance requirements, including those that might require them to transfer technology, merge or form alliances with local enterprises, hire local employees, or purchase local inputs.

- invest without fear that host governments might nationalize or regulate their operations in ways that reduce their profitability.

Though history demonstrates that transnational capital does not require such guarantees to expand its international division of labor, it is easy to see why it finds them attractive, given the growing importance of cross-border production activity. In fact, an average of two bilateral investment treaties were signed every week over the decade ending in 2007. As of 2007, there were approximately 250 agreements in effect, covering more than 50 percent of world trade.[12]

As we saw in chapter 1, FTAs have become especially popular in East Asia, helping to provide a critical infrastructure for transnational capital's East Asian cross-border production activity. At the same time, most participating countries have also pursued agreements with countries outside the region. They did so for two reasons. First, countries hosting cross-border networks are under constant pressure to attract foreign investment from and secure open trade relationships with as many countries as possible. This is especially true for China, since it serves as the final assembly platform for the region's exports.

Second, many of East Asia's more developed countries—in particular, Japan, Korea, and Singapore—host powerful transnational corporations whose operations are not limited to participation in existing production networks or whose exports may compete with those produced by companies that do. Their governments need to ensure an attractive export environment or risk losing these corporations.

The KORUS Agreement: Motivations and Negotiations

The developments described above provide important context for explaining Korean and U.S. government motivations for pursuing their own bilateral FTA. For its part, the Korean government feared that East Asia's expanding network of export production would continue to draw investment out of Korea, further weakening the country's manufacturing base. Therefore, it initiated FTA negotiations with the United States. Korean capitalists eagerly supported this initiative, hoping to gain preferential access to the U.S. market before China and Japan.

The Korean government had entered into FTA negotiations with Japan in 2002, but those talks failed. The main reason was that Korean manufacturers did not support an agreement with Japan. This experience illustrates two important, although obvious, points. First, capitalists do not blindly favor FTAs; they support only those that they believe serve their interests. And second, agreements are unlikely to be completed without their support. As Mi Park explained:

> Korean capital pressured the government to sign an FTA with the United States, while opposing an FTA with Japan. Since the proposed FTA with Japan was regarded as disadvantageous to Korea, the negotiations with Japan reached a deadlock in 2005. Although agricultural issues were ostensibly the source of disagreement, the real reason was that Korea had a comparative disadvantage in the areas where Korean capital had a big stake. Korean capital felt that, given the similar economic structures of the two countries (both are export-oriented economies with a major focus on autos and electronics), Korean capital would lose out from an FTA due to Japan's superior technology. [Both] Samsung electronics and . . . the national lobby group of Korean capital opposed the FTA and consequently, the FTA negotiations broke down. Korean capital saw more potential gains from an FTA with the United States, given the different economic structure of the two countries (strong agricultural and service sectors in the United States versus a strong manufacturing sector in Korea). As a result, Korean capital believed that an FTA with the United States would provide greater opportunities for the sale

of cars and electronic goods in the U.S. markets. Thus, when the Korean government entered into FTA negotiations with the United States, it worked closely with business think tanks to ensure that Korean capital's interests would be protected.[13]

The U.S. government was not a reluctant negotiating partner. It feared that the country was losing economic influence in East Asia, especially to China. Both government and business leaders viewed an agreement with Korea as an excellent way to begin rebalancing economic relations with East Asia for three main reasons. First, Korea's military-political dependence on the United States gave the U.S. government an enormous negotiating advantage.[14] Second, an agreement with Korea would help counter China's growing economic influence in Korea, thereby demonstrating the determination and ability of the United States to remain a significant economic player in all of East Asia. Third, leading U.S. financial service companies were eager to gain entrance into Korea's relatively large but protected financial service market.

Taking advantage of Korea's dependence, the U.S. government demanded that the Korean government meet their conditions before it would even agree to start talks. These required the Korean government to change its laws to make it easier for U.S. companies to sell their drugs, cars, movies, and beef in Korea.[15] Not long after the last condition was met, the two governments publicly announced that negotiations would start in May 2006 and be completed by June 2007. The negotiations actually concluded in April 2007, and Korean and U.S. trade representatives signed the final agreement on June 30, 2007.[16]

Although political leaders in both countries were optimistic that their legislatures would quickly approve the agreement, it was not to be. Almost immediately, the U.S. Congress, responding to strong pressure from beef and automobile interests, demanded changes. In response, the Korean government agreed to a 2008 side deal that further opened Korean markets to U.S. beef imports, despite popular concerns about mad cow disease. The deal triggered major protests and demonstrations that almost toppled the Korean government.

Regardless, congressional opponents continued to claim that the agreement did not do enough to protect U.S. jobs. Several automobile producers, as well as the United Auto Workers (UAW), were especially vocal in demanding renegotiation of the part of the agreement dealing with cars and light trucks (including SUVs). With the Korean president and leaders of the Korean National Assembly adamant that they would accept no further changes, it appeared that ratification would never take place.

However, the KORUS FTA found its way back onto the U.S. political agenda. Under intense pressure to boost employment, President Obama in January 2010 called for doubling exports over the next five years, an increase, he claimed, that would create 2 million jobs. Achieving this goal, he added, required, among other things, approval of the three FTAs that had been negotiated but not yet ratified by Congress—those with Korea, Colombia, and Panama.

To speed the process, President Obama pressed Korea to accept yet another change in the agreement, this time regarding the trade in autos and light trucks. In December 2010, after months of negotiating, the Korean government finally agreed.[17] Originally, the United States was to eliminate its 2.5 percent tariff on imports of Korean cars and phase out (over a ten-year period) its 25 percent tariff on Korean light trucks and SUVs. In return, Korea was to eliminate its 8 percent tariff on U.S. auto imports and its 10 percent tariff on imports of U.S. light trucks and SUVs.[18]

U.S. automakers, especially Ford, and the UAW had argued that whereas cutting U.S. tariffs would enable Korean auto companies to sell more cars and light trucks in the U.S. market, Korean tariff cuts, though larger, would not be as helpful to U.S. companies. The reason was that a variety of non-tariff barriers involving tax policies and fuel, emission, and safety standards would continue to restrict U.S. exports to Korea.[19]

The changes the Korean government agreed to represented a minor but real concession. The new terms allowed the United

States to delay its tariff reduction on Korean cars for five years and maintain its existing light truck tariff rate for eight years (rather than gradually reduce it). The Korean government also agreed to raise the number of U.S. cars that could be imported without meeting Korean safety standards from 6,500 vehicles per year per automaker to 25,000. It also agreed to new "transparency rules" that lengthened the time automakers had to comply with new regulations and created a review system to ensure that new regulations would not be trade discriminatory.

These changes were sufficient to win Ford's endorsement of the KORUS FTA. Perhaps more important politically, they also satisfied the UAW leadership.[20] Shortly after completion of the renegotiation, Ron Kirk, the U.S. trade representative, claimed that "the tariff cuts alone in the U.S.-Korea trade agreement will increase exports of American goods and services [to Korea] by $10 to $11 billion. We expect this agreement to create 70,000-plus jobs for American workers in a wide range of economic sectors, from autos and manufacturing to agriculture."[21]

As we will see below, this claim is not supportable. The truth is that the U.S. government had no idea what this agreement would mean as far as jobs were concerned. Regardless, the claim was useful for providing an effective ideological cover for an agreement that is profoundly anti-worker.

The KORUS FTA is best understood as a deal between Korean and U.S. economic elites. Korea's dominant manufacturers—especially those producing automobiles, ships, semiconductors, telecommunication equipment, and steel—want greater access to the U.S. market. Leading U.S. financial service companies (as well as agricultural and pharmaceutical companies) want greater access to the Korean market. Each group is willing to open its national economy to the other because each has different market interests.

As a result, this agreement will, by design, reinforce economic dynamics in both countries that are desperately in need of change. The Korean economy has become ever more dependent on the exports of its leading manufacturers. Exports in the first half of

2008 accounted for approximately 65 percent of GDP, a record high at the time; it has moved considerably higher since.[22] To support this export activity, the Korean state has aggressively restructured labor markets. The percentage of workers with irregular labor status has accordingly grown from approximately 40 percent before 2000 to over 60 percent by 2008. These workers earn little more than half of what regular workers earn in monthly wages.[23] Ratification of the KORUS FTA can be expected to intensify these economic and social trends.

The U.S. economy has become increasingly dependent on the activity of its leading financial service firms; from the mid-1980s to the late 2000s, financial profits grew from less than 20 percent of total corporate profits to almost 40 percent.[24] Financial profits fell sharply during the Great Recession, but quickly rebounded in the following years. The financialization of the U.S. economy greatly contributed to the growth of poverty and inequality, mounting debt, and the crisis that continues to plague working people in the United States. By strengthening the dominant position of leading U.S. financial service firms, this agreement will only make it harder to overcome existing economic imbalances and related social problems.

KORUS FTA Content and Consequences: Tariff Liberalization

The KORUS FTA, like other FTAs, is composed of two basic parts. The first details the tariff reductions that each country must make. The second prescribes the restrictions to be placed on the ability of governments to regulate corporate activity. Though both parts provide advantages to the most dynamic corporations in each country, Korean corporations stand to benefit most from the first part, broadly speaking, and U.S. corporations can be expected to benefit disproportionately from the second part.

Most discussions of the KORUS FTA focus on the first part, the extent and consequences of the agreement's mandated tariff liberalization. According to the United States International Trade

Commission (USITC), the KORUS FTA (as originally negotiated in 2007)

> will eliminate duties on a wide range of the partner countries' originating goods immediately, while phasing out duties on other originating goods over differing transition periods and providing for preferential TRQs [tariff rate quotas] on certain sensitive (primarily agricultural) goods. The United States and Korean tariff schedules (with annexes and notes) cover all goods.... Whereas 38 percent of the U.S. tariff lines are already free of duty, only 13 percent are so for Korea. Of the more than 10,600 U.S. and 11,200 Korean tariff lines, approximately 82 percent of U.S. tariff lines and approximately 80 percent of Korean tariff lines would have free rates of duty (currently and immediately free of duty) upon entry into force of the FTA. Approximately 93 percent of U.S. tariff lines and 92 percent of Korean tariff lines would have free rates of duty after 5 years; and approximately 99 percent of U.S. tariff lines and 98 percent of Korean tariff lines would have free rates of duty by year 10.[25]

The argument U.S. officials made is that since Korea has more goods covered by tariffs than the United States, the tariff reductions the agreement mandates will disproportionately benefit the U.S. economy. This argument is often buttressed by reference to the theory of comparative advantage, which purports to demonstrate that free trade will produce benefits for both parties, regardless of their level of development.[26] Of course, as noted above, the U.S. government offers more than a theoretical defense of the KORUS FTA, claiming that it will produce a $10 to $11 billion increase in U.S. exports to Korea, which will support the creation of approximately 70,000 new jobs. But where do those figures come from?

The USITC provides official estimates of the economic impact of the agreement by employing a global computable general equilibrium (CGE) model. It was this model that generated the increase in U.S. exports to Korea. Things become less clear-cut from this point. Apparently, Kirk decided to use International Trade Administration estimates that every $150,000 in exports supports one U.S. job. Applying this multiplier to the predicted increase in exports gives a range of 73,333 to 66,667 jobs. As noted in the *Eyes on Trade Blog*: "The 70,000 jobs stat is right in the middle of the range, so there is a high probability that this is the origin of the estimate."[27]

However, this estimate does not take into account the effect of imports on employment. If one assumes that an increase in exports will create jobs, one must also assume that an increase in imports will reduce them. Taking the import effects into account erases approximately 60 percent of the projected job gains.[28]

Kirk also conveniently overlooked the fact that USITC modeling involves the entire world. In other words, the USITC recognizes that changes in U.S. and Korean tariff rates will affect trade flows between the United States and other countries as well as with Korea. It therefore provides estimates for U.S. trade outcomes with these other countries in addition to its estimates for Korea. As it turns out, approximately half of the U.S. export increase to Korea is the result of trade diversion rather than new exports.[29]

There are additional reasons to reject the Obama administration's defense of the KORUS FTA. Perhaps the most significant is that the estimates of the economic effects of this and other trade agreements made by the USITC (and other researchers) are based on a flawed methodology; this problem reveals, in stark terms, the class nature of contemporary economic thinking and its role in mystifying capitalist accumulation dynamics.

As noted above, the USITC used a global CGE model to generate its estimates. CGE models define national economies as a collection of interconnected markets. When prices change—in this case because of tariff changes—national product markets are assumed to adjust to restore equilibrium. Since economies are themselves connected through trade, price changes are also assumed to generate more complex global adjustments before a new equilibrium outcome is achieved.

As we saw in chapter 2, this type of modeling is challenging. For example, it requires specific estimates of consumer and producer behavior in different markets and in different nations, including their speed of adjustment. USITC researchers relied upon the Global Trade Analysis Project (GTAP) for their basic model and data. The GTAP "consists of a global database on international trade, economy-wide inter-industry relationships, and national income accounts (the GTAP database), and a standard modeling framework to organize and analyze the data (the GTAP model)."[30] The USITC adjusted both the GTAP model and database, updating and reorganizing the data to create 10 "economies" and 54 sectors.

On the basis of such modeling, the USITC concluded, in addition to its export prediction, that adoption of the KORUS FTA would likely increase U.S. GDP by $10.1 to $11.9 billion, which is basically a rounding error in an economy with a $14.5 trillion GDP, and that "employment changes would likely be negligible."[31] Other researchers also used CGE modeling to estimate the effects of the KORUS FTA, and their studies produced similar results.[32]

In short, we have a general consensus within the economics profession about how to model trade agreements and a general consensus among those that have modeled this specific agreement about its likely consequences. But how much confidence should we have in their "empirically supported" endorsement of the KORUS FTA? The answer is very little, if any.

The primary reason is that CGE modeling requires assumptions that heavily bias its results in favor of free trade. These assumptions generally include the following:

- There are just two inputs, capital and labor. Though these inputs are perfectly malleable and able to move instantaneously between sectors in each country, they never cross national borders.
- Total aggregate expenditure in each economy will be sufficient, and automatically adjust, to ensure full employment of all resources.

- Flexible exchange rates will prevent tariff changes from causing changes in trade balances.

Said differently, this kind of modeling assumes a world in which liberalization cannot, by assumption, cause or worsen unemployment, capital flight, or trade imbalances. Thanks to these assumptions, if a country drops its trade restrictions, market forces will quickly and effortlessly lead capital and labor to shift into new, more productive uses. And since trade always remains in balance, this restructuring will generate a dollar's worth of new exports for every dollar's worth of new imports. Given these assumptions, it is no wonder that mainstream economic studies always produce results supporting ratification of free trade agreements.

Ironically, Kozo Kiyota and Robert M. Stern, two well-known international trade economists, confidently draw on the results of their own CGE modeling to support ratification of the KORUS FTA, despite their own warning about the danger of using CGE modeling for predictive purposes. As they explained:

> It is important to understand that the CGE modeling simulation results provide indications of the potential economic changes involved. In this respect, they are not meant to be empirical forecasts or predictions of the changes because they are not derived from econometric methods that can yield statistically based estimations. Further, because they are microeconomic in character, CGE models of necessity abstract from the macroeconomic forces at work at the aggregate level in individual countries. As a consequence, it may be very difficult to compare CGE modeling results with the actual changes that occur in the economic variables over given periods of time.[33]

This brief assessment of mainstream economic methodology leads to the conclusion that the claims this methodology generates should not be taken as the basis for policy decisions—they are far more the result of free-market ideology than serious scientific inquiry.[34] This conclusion should encourage us to consider alternative methodologies, especially those that take seriously our actual experience with three decades of policies promoting the liberalization and deregulation of economic activity, including trade. Contrary to mainstream assertions, this experience has certainly not been positive in terms of either economic growth or job creation. In fact, liberalization has been associated with the opposite.[35]

A study by Robert Scott, which does draw on past experience to study the likely economic effects of the KORUS FTA, finds that the agreement will be harmful.[36] Scott first calculated compound annual growth rates of U.S. trade flows (imports and exports) with Mexico and China seven years before and after implementation of NAFTA and China's entry into the WTO. He then determined the differences in the pre- and post-trade agreement rates of growth of imports and exports between Mexico and the United States, and between China and the United States. He averaged the results from both cases to get an average change in post-agreement U.S. trade activity: the post-agreement growth rate in U.S. imports was 5.1 percentage points higher than the pre-agreement rate; the post-agreement growth rate in U.S. exports was 2.8 percentage points higher than the pre-agreement rate.[37] Finally, he used these average differences to estimate the likely consequences of the KORUS FTA. Scott's work yielded a predicted $13.5 billion increase in the U.S. trade deficit with Korea and an expected decline of 159,000 U.S. jobs over the years 2008 to 2015.[38]

Adding credence to Scott's work, *Public Citizen* compared the U.S. trade record with 17 FTA partners with the trade record with non-FTA partners. It found that between 1998 and 2008, "the growth of U.S. exports to countries that are not FTA partners is as much as double the growth of exports to U.S. FTA partners."[39]

This discussion of economic modeling reinforces a key point made earlier, namely that the likely consequences of a trade agreement cannot be understood in isolation from national economic dynamics. In other words, trade policy is best understood as a logical extension of existing national patterns of economic activity and as such can be expected to reinforce those patterns.

For example, CGE modeling assumes the existence of an idealized capitalist economy. As a result, market forces are expected to produce full employment and the most efficient distribution of resources and organization of production possible. Given these conditions, the only way to improve on this outcome is to widen the scope of the market. By allowing global market forces to shape exchanges between nations, each nation's factors of production (which by assumption always remain within their country of origin and fully employed) will be allocated more efficiently, resulting in even greater specialization and output.

However, if we assume a different capitalist economy—one dominated by powerful firms that use their power to control markets and exploit workers and the natural environment to maximize profits—a free trade agreement would likely have different consequences. Rather than a more socially productive use of resources, the enhanced corporate mobility would likely produce a broadening and intensification of socially destructive trends. This understanding helps to explain why free trade agreements produce outcomes far different from those predicted by mainstream economists.

KORUS FTA Content and Consequences: Limiting Public Power

Despite its name, the KORUS FTA has a second part, one that involves issues largely unrelated to simple trade liberalization. Popular belief in free trade is strong, therefore cloaking the agreement in terms of "freeing" trade is one way for its supporters to present it as a noncontroversial effort to improve popular welfare. The KORUS FTA has twenty-four chapters, including the twenty listed below. Almost all of these chapters are primarily designed to free corporate activity from state regulation:

- National Treatment and Market Access for Goods
- Agriculture
- Textiles and Apparel
- Pharmaceuticals and Medical Devices
- Rules of Origin and Origin Procedures
- Sanitary and Phytosanitary Measures
- Technical Barriers to Trade
- Trade Remedies
- Investment
- Cross-Border Trade in Services
- Financial Services
- Telecommunications
- Electronic Commerce
- Competition-Related Matters
- Government Procurement
- Intellectual Property Rights
- Labor
- Environment
- Transparency
- Institutional Provisions and Dispute Settlement

To fully appreciate the ways in which the KORUS FTA serves corporate interests at public expense, I highlight the contents of three of these chapters—Government Procurement, Financial Services, and Investment.

THE GOVERNMENT PROCUREMENT CHAPTER

The Government Procurement chapter includes restrictions that greatly limit the ability of governments (at all levels) to promote or direct economic activity in the public interest. The chapter covers all government purchases for public purposes "of goods, services, or any combination thereof . . . by any contractual means, including purchase; lease; rental or hire purchase, with or without an option to buy; build-operate-transfer contracts; and public works concession contracts . . . for which the value equals or exceeds the relevant threshold."⁴⁰

Under the terms of the agreement, governments must "limit any conditions for participation in a procurement to those that are essential to ensure that a supplier has the legal and financial capacities and the commercial and technical abilities to undertake the relevant procurement."⁴¹ This requirement means, for example, that when governments choose a contractor, they cannot take into account its past labor or environmental record. They also cannot require a contractor to use local workers and/or locally produced goods or services. Governments can buy only from the company that offers the lowest price, assuming the firm is financially viable and technically capable of fulfilling the contract.

In addition, governments cannot adopt technical specifications that "lay down the characteristics of the products or services to be procured, such as quality, performance, safety and dimensions, symbols, terminology, packaging, marking and labeling, or the processes and methods for their production and requirements relating to conformity assessment procedures prescribed by procuring entities" if they have the intent or effect of "creating unnecessary obstacles to international trade."⁴² This means that governments would largely be forbidden from including requirements in their procurement contracts that specify how a good is made or a service is provided, even if there is no intention of privileging a domestic over foreign provider.

As the Labor Advisory Committee for Trade Negotiations and Trade Policy pointed out, though "Article 7 provides an exception for technical specifications to promote the conservation of natural resources or protect the environment, numerous other public interest regulations could still be challenged."⁴³ Indeed, it is possible that living wage agreements could be found illegal under the terms of this chapter.

In short, the Government Procurement chapter goes a long way toward ensuring that public authorities will be unable to use public money in ways that might interfere with corporate profit maximization. Although the terms of this agreement cover only biddings in the United States that involve Korean companies, or biddings in Korea that involve U.S. companies, in reality governments in both countries will find themselves forced to adopt these terms for all procurement activity by all firms, or risk putting their own corporations at a disadvantage. The result will be a significant extension of corporate power at public expense.

THE FINANCIAL SERVICES CHAPTER

As noted above, the financial service sector was a driving force in shaping the U.S. negotiating position, and financial firms clearly succeeded in getting an agreement responsive to their interests. Citigroup's Laura Lane, corporate co-chair of the U.S.-Korea FTA Business Coalition, declared that the KORUS FTA had "the best financial services chapter negotiated in a free trade agreement to date."[44]

For example, under the terms of this chapter, governments cannot

> adopt or maintain, with respect to financial institutions of the other Party or investors of the other Party seeking to establish such institutions . . . measures that impose limitations on the number of financial institutions, . . . the total value of financial service transactions or assets, . . . or the total number of financial service operations or on the total quantity of financial services output."[45]

Governments are also forbidden from adopting measures that "restrict or require specific types of legal entity or joint venture through which a financial institution may supply a service."[46]

Covered financial services include activities related to all forms of insurance, including insurance intermediation (such as brokerage and agency) and services auxiliary to insurance (such as consultancy, actuarial, risk assessment, and claim settlement services). Also covered are activities related to banking and other financial services, including acceptance of deposits; lending of all types; financial leasing; payment and money transmission services (such as those involving credit, charge and debit cards, traveler's checks, and banker's drafts); trading whether on an exchange, in an over-the-counter market, or otherwise; assets such as money market instruments, foreign exchange, derivatives, exchange rate and interest rate instruments, and transferable securities; money broking; asset management—and the list goes on.[47]

These restrictions mean that governments would be unable to limit the size of foreign financial service firms or covered financial activities. More specifically, governments would be unable to ensure that financial institutions do not grow "too big to fail," a concern of many U.S. financial regulators. They would also be unable to limit various speculative activities, such as derivative trading.

In addition, these restrictions would outlaw the use of capital controls, since such controls restrict flows of funds seeking or fleeing investment opportunities. In 2010, the Korean government imposed controls that limited the Korean financial assets that foreign investors could purchase in an effort to maintain currency stability.[48] If this agreement were ratified, a U.S. financial service company operating in Korea could force the Korean government to rescind these controls.

And, because governments would be unable to limit the total number of financial service operations undertaken by a financial services firm, they would also be unable to ensure a separation of activities. As a consequence, the United States could be legally blocked from employing measures such as the Depression-era Glass-Steagall Act or the proposed Volcker Rule, which are designed to create firewalls between different types of financial activities.[49] In short, the Financial Services chapter bans the use of many important regulations even if they were applied equally to domestic and foreign firms.

Additionally, the chapter limits the ability of governments to ensure the confidentiality of consumer information. The U.S. Coalition of Service Industries had long complained that Korean laws designed to protect consumer privacy limited the ability of foreign companies operating in Korea to offshore their data-processing activities.[50] The Coalition wanted, and did finally gain, the right for U.S. financial service companies to transfer Korean data across national borders. The KORUS FTA includes a provision, not found in other agreements, that says, "Each Party shall allow a financial institution of the other Party to transfer information in electronic or other form, into and out of its territory, for data processing where such processing is required in the institution's ordinary course of business."[51]

The chapter does contain "prudential measures" language, which is supposed to ensure that the Korean and U.S. governments will be able to take whatever actions they deem necessary to protect the financial stability of their respective economies. However, the language of the KORUS FTA prudential measures "defense" is ambiguous. It reads:

> A Party shall not be prevented from adopting or maintaining measures for prudential reasons, including for the protection of investors, depositors, policy holders, or persons to whom a fiduciary duty is owed by a financial institution or cross-border financial service supplier, or to ensure the integrity and stability of the financial system. Where such measures do not conform with the provisions of this Agreement referred to in this paragraph, they shall not be used as a means of avoiding the Party's commitments or obligations under such provisions.[52]

As *Public Citizen* explained,

> This self-cancelling language undermines the use of the defense to actually protect a financial regulation: a country would only need to use this provision if its domestic policy did

not conform with the agreement. In other words, a country would only be challenged because it undermined an obligation that a foreign firm or government believed was provided in the pact. To restate, this circular defense measure does not provide a reliable safeguard.[53]

Finally, the chapter incorporates the investor-state enforcement mechanism established in the Investment chapter (discussed next), which allows U.S. financial firms or investors operating in Korea the right to directly sue the Korean government, and Korean firms and investors operating in the United States the right to directly sue the U.S. government, if these firms or investors feel that public regulations are abridging their rights. Moreover, depending on the wishes of these foreign firms and investors, these suits could be heard in international tribunals whose rulings would supersede existing national laws.

Though the Financial Services chapter does not give firms or investors the right to sue their own government, or firms or investors from a third country the right to sue either the Korean or U.S. governments, it appears that there is a loophole in the agreement that would make this possible. According to *Public Citizen*, "Korean subsidiaries of U.S. (or Chinese or European) banks and securities firms may well have standing to challenge U.S. laws in foreign tribunals."[54]

THE INVESTMENT CHAPTER

The Investment chapter of the KORUS FTA establishes broad limits on the ability of governments (at all levels) to regulate or restrict private profit-seeking investments by foreign investors. Investments covered include

> every asset that an investor owns or controls, directly or indirectly, that has the characteristics of an investment, including

such characteristics as the commitment of capital or other resources, the expectation of gain or profit, or the assumption of risk. Forms that an investment may take include:

a) an enterprise;
b) shares, stock, and other forms of equity participation in an enterprise;
c) bonds, debentures, other debt instruments, and loans;
d) futures, options, and other derivatives;
e) turnkey, construction, management, production, concession, revenue sharing, and other similar contracts;
f) intellectual property rights;
g) licenses, authorizations, permits, and similar rights conferred pursuant to domestic law; and
h) other tangible or intangible, movable or immovable property, and related property rights, such as leases, mortgages, liens, and pledges.[55]

This chapter is supposed to secure the protection of Korean investors in the United States and U.S. investors in Korea. In actuality, it will ensure that Korean and U.S. investors enjoy these protections in their own countries as well. Although this agreement allows governments to offer foreign investors protections that exceed those they offer to their own investors, it is highly unlikely they will do so. Thus the freedoms granted to foreign investors under the terms of this chapter will sooner or later be extended to domestic firms as well. And since a wide range of activities are to be protected under the terms of this chapter, it is likely that many corporations will benefit from them.

One protection granted to foreign corporations is the freedom from government-imposed performance requirements. According to the chapter:

Neither Party may, in connection with the establishment, acquisition, expansion, management, conduct, operation, or

sale or other disposition of an investment in its territory of an
investor of a Party or of a non-Party, impose or enforce any
requirement or enforce any commitment or undertaking:

a) to export a given level or percentage of goods or services;
b) to achieve a given level or percentage of domestic content;
c) to purchase, use, or accord a preference to goods produced in its territory, or to purchase goods from persons
   in its territory;
d) to relate in any way the volume or value of imports to the
   volume or value of exports or to the amount of foreign
   exchange inflows associated with such investment;
e) to restrict sales of goods or services in its territory that
   such investment produces or supplies by relating such
   sales in any way to the volume or value of its exports or
   foreign exchange earnings;
f) to transfer a particular technology, a production process, or
   other proprietary knowledge to a person in its territory; or
g) to supply exclusively from the territory of the Party the
   goods that such investment produces or the services that
   it supplies to a specific regional market or to the world
   market.[56]

This protection clearly limits the ability of a government to
implement any meaningful industrial policy.

The Investment chapter also gives foreign corporations protection from expropriation. More specifically, "Neither Party may
expropriate or nationalize a covered investment either directly
or indirectly through measures equivalent to expropriation or
nationalization."[57] Critical here is the notion of indirect expropriation or nationalization.

Indirect expropriation refers to a government action or regulation that has "an effect equivalent to direct expropriation without
formal transfer of title or outright seizure."[58] A direct nationalization is relatively easy to define, since it involves an outright

government seizure of title and/or assets. Determining whether an indirect nationalization has occurred is far more difficult. In the words of the chapter, such a determination will require

> a case-by-case, fact-based inquiry that considers all relevant factors relating to the investment, including:
>
> i)   the economic impact of the government action, although the fact that an action or a series of actions by a Party has an adverse effect on the economic value of an investment, standing alone, does not establish that an indirect expropriation has occurred;
>
> ii) the extent to which the government action interferes with distinct, reasonable investment-backed expectations; and
>
> iii) the character of the government action, including its objectives and context. Relevant considerations could include whether the government action imposes a special sacrifice on the particular investor or investment that exceeds what the investor or investment should be expected to endure for the public interest.[59]

Given the broad range of covered investments, this definition means that many government actions could conceivably result in an indirect expropriation from the perspective of the investor. This is especially true given that an investor can claim an indirect expropriation if, as noted above, a government action "interferes with distinct, reasonable investment-backed expectations" or "imposes a special sacrifice on the particular investor or investment that exceeds what the investor or investment should be expected to endure for the public interest."

The Investment chapter offers a framework for considering when a corporation might have reasonable cause to argue that a government action caused it harm. The text says:

> For greater certainty, whether an investor's investment-backed expectations are reasonable depends in part on the nature and

extent of governmental regulation in the relevant sector. For example, an investor's expectations that regulations will not change are less likely to be reasonable in a heavily regulated sector than in a less heavily regulated sector.[60]

There is enough ambiguity in all of this that one can easily imagine foreign corporations challenging many government regulations. And if a corporation does feel that it is the victim of an indirect expropriation, the chapter gives it the power to directly sue the unit of government that has implemented the offending rule or regulation. Under the terms of the investor-state dispute settlement mechanism, the investor can have a claim judged under the International Centre for Settlement of Investment Disputes (ICSID) Convention and Rules of Procedure for Arbitration, the United Nations Commission on International Trade Law Arbitration Rules, or any other system of arbitration if it is agreed to by both parties.

If the ICSID is chosen to judge the claim, which has been the most common choice of investors under international treaties, three arbitrators will be selected from a list of international trade and investment specialists. Each side selects one, with a third chosen by agreement of the two sides. In other words, this dispute settlement mechanism allows a corporation to challenge a governmental action outside the legal system of the host nation.[61]

Thanks to NAFTA, which has a similar investor–state dispute settlement mechanism, we have an example of how this process works. In 1996, the Loewen Group, a Canadian funeral home company, lost a $500 million verdict to a Mississippi funeral home business that had accused it of fraudulent business practices. Loewen appealed the case to the Mississippi Supreme Court, which refused to overturn the decision. In 1999, the Loewen Group took its case to a NAFTA tribunal, arguing that the verdict against the company should be invalidated because the court proceedings were tainted by anti-Canadian bias. Loewen asked the tribunal for compensation for what it had to pay to settle the case and for additional damages to compensate the company for the harm done to its business reputation.[62]

The tribunal issued its decision in 2003, ruling in favor of the United States. The *Dispute Resolution Journal* described the reasoning and conclusions of the tribunal as follows:

> In its 71-page award, the tribunal . . . acknowledged that this was a difficult case. The award addressed the Loewen Group's claims of an unfair process as well as the United States' numerous arguments that it was not liable under NAFTA. In so doing, the tribunal chronicled the injustices suffered by the company and its founder, co-claimant Raymond Loewen. Ultimately, it found, among other things, that "the conduct of the trial judge was so flawed as to constitute a miscarriage of justice amounting to a manifest injustice as that expression is understood in international law." The tribunal also said that the jury verdict was grossly excessive to the amounts in dispute and therefore the claimants had "strong prospects" of a successful appeal. . . .
>
> After recounting its findings, the tribunal explained that its decision to dismiss the NAFTA claims on the merits was ultimately based on a lack of jurisdiction. It reasoned that it had no authority to determine the Loewen Group's NAFTA claims because the company had reorganized under Chapter 11 of the Bankruptcy Code as an American corporation and then assigned its NAFTA claims to a newly formed Canadian corporation "owned and controlled by an American corporation." NAFTA, the tribunal pointed out, was not intended to address investment-related claims by domestic investors against their government.[63]

In other words, the tribunal found it within its authority to rule on this case, even though its decision could potentially overturn a decision made by a U.S. court. And it gave strong indication that it felt such action was justified by its reading of the submitted documents. The tribunal rejected the claim only because the Loewen Group, by reorganizing itself as a U.S.-registered company, was no longer a "foreign" company and thus no longer had standing under the terms of NAFTA. If the tribunal had ruled in Loewen's favor, the U.S. government would have been forced to compensate the company. It seems safe to say that the terms would create an environment in which governments would understandably be leery of doing anything that might be viewed as harmful to corporate profitability, present or future.

In sum, the three KORUS FTA chapters discussed above (and others not considered here) involve far more than trade liberalization as commonly understood.[64] They are, at root, designed to strengthen corporate power by legislating restrictions on the freedom of action of public agencies. Significantly, and worth emphasizing, it was the governments of Korea and the United States that negotiated this agreement on behalf of their respective leading corporations.

No wonder that government and business leaders prefer to call the KORUS FTA a free trade agreement and to concentrate public attention on tariff issues. If the full requirements of this and other agreements were popularly known, people might better understand why they face ever worsening options.[65] They would see that their situation is primarily the result of well applied class power rather than impersonal "market forces." And they would better appreciate the need to organize in their own defense.

Defeating the KORUS FTA: Evaluating Strategies

As argued above, the KORUS FTA does not serve U.S. (or Korean) majority interests. The same is true for U.S. agreements with Colombia and Panama. However, given that major business and political leaders strongly supported these agreements, defeat of them required sustained organizing and movement-building activities designed to help people grasp their true significance.

More specifically, in organizing against the KORUS FTA, the aim had to be making transparent the connection between the specifics of the agreement and the underlying class interests of those who shaped it and continue to promote it.

Establishing this connection helps demonstrate that this agreement is more than a complex legal document whose interpretation is best left to the judgment of experts. It also lays the groundwork for demonstrating that, despite their many differences, all FTAs have a common taproot in capitalist imperatives. In this way, insights gained in resisting the KORUS FTA can quickly and logically be transformed into opposition to other FTAs, and finally to an awareness of the need to work for the structural transformation of the U.S. economy itself.

In many ways, capitalism is like the mythical Hydra of Greek legend, a gigantic serpent with multiple heads, the center one being immortal. Every time an attacker chopped off one of the hydra's outer heads, two others grew in its place. It was finally killed by Heracles with the assistance of his charioteer Iolaus. As Heracles chopped off a head, Iolaus would burn its neck cavity to keep new heads from growing. Eventually they reached the center head, which Heracles severed from its body and buried deep in the ground, with a huge boulder placed on top. Capitalism resembles the hydra in that its dynamics generate multiple trade agreements, all of which work to promote the expansion of private profit-making activities regardless of their social, economic, political, and environmental costs. The ongoing tensions generated by capitalism ensure that new "heads" are always in formation.

Capitalism is also like the hydra in that it is not easily overcome. Reform attempts directed at its individual "heads" are rarely able to produce lasting benefits. For example, in response to the growth of internationally structured production, governments began negotiating free trade agreements. When they were frustrated in their attempts to conclude multilateral ones, they turned to bilateral ones. If these become difficult to negotiate, they will, no doubt, pursue regional ones. Therefore, what is needed is a political strategy that uses each struggle against an individual agreement to build a larger movement directed at transforming capitalism itself. It is this understanding that was needed to shape resistance to the KORUS FTA.

Unfortunately many of the efforts groups and organizations in the United States made to defeat the KORUS FTA did not encourage this broader political development. In fact, some were actually counterproductive. Many U.S. critics of the KORUS FTA accepted the U.S. government's claim that the agreement is primarily about tariff reduction and should be judged in terms of its ability to promote job-creating exports. They parted ways with the government only because they did not believe that the agreement, as structured, was capable of achieving this goal. For most, the problem is that our government is naïve—it did not negotiate hard enough to ensure that the Korean government will play by the same free-market rules we do.

For example, Scott, writing for the progressive Economic Policy Institute, argued against ratification of the agreement largely on the grounds that Korea is not a fair trader. As a result, though tariff reductions will enable Korean firms to sell more to the United States, they will do little to help U.S. firms sell more to Korea. As he explained:

> Although Korea has agreed to phase out trade restrictions for many products and services in the U.S.-Korea FTA, Korea maintains substantial non-tariff barriers to trade, and it has also maintained a network of subsidies for target industries. Overall, the Korean trade regime bears many similarities to that of China. China agreed to eliminate nominal barriers to imports such as tariffs and non-tariff barriers to trade as part of the agreements it signed as a condition for WTO entry and permanent normal trade relations with the United States. However, after China was admitted to the WTO in 2001 it maintained and expanded many of these trade barriers and erected new ones so as to develop a very large and growing trade surplus.[66]

Scott also singled out Korea's currency management as another example of inappropriate government intervention. Korea, again like China, refuses to allow market forces to set the rate of its currency. Without the "sustained purchases of foreign exchange," the "growing demand for the Korean won would have resulted in higher levels of currency appreciation, which would have made imports cheaper and Korea's exports more expensive, thus likely resulting in a Korean trade deficit throughout much of this period, something which would apparently have been unacceptable to Korean leaders."[67]

Scott's arguments against the KORUS FTA carry a political message: we are engaged in a national competition and our government needs to be tougher about making sure that Korea increases its reliance on market forces. His arguments may have persuaded working people to oppose this agreement, but the victory comes at a high price. It encourages people to see "free market" capitalism as the desired form of economic organization and, by extension, free trade agreements as a potentially attractive instrument for defending U.S. economic interests.

Most union leaders and activists shared Scott's concern that the agreement, as negotiated, did not adequately protect U.S. producers and employment. For some, the only issue is "jobs." Unfortunately, this narrow focus meant that little popular attention was given to the critical issues raised by the various chapters of the agreement. In fact, their criticisms of the KORUS FTA were rarely, if ever, directed at the overall aims of the agreement, which were generally treated as noble. Rather they sought improvements in the terms and timing of the trade liberalization effort.

The decision by the UAW leadership to endorse the KORUS FTA offers a good example of the dangerous consequences of this limited critique. Initially, the UAW strongly opposed the agreement. As discussed above, it believed that Korea's numerous non-tariff trade barriers meant that the U.S. auto industry and autoworkers would gain little from the mandated tariff reductions. It was also concerned about the agreement's low "rules of origin": only 35 percent of the components used to manufacture a product have to come from one of the two countries to be eligible for preferential treatment.[68] The UAW leadership feared that Korean car producers would gain market share in the United States by selling cars largely assembled with cheap components sourced in China.[69]

However, after the Korean government agreed in December 2010 to relax Korean fuel, emission, and safety standards for U.S. cars and accept a delay in U.S. tariff reductions on Korean auto and small truck imports, the UAW declared its support for the agreement. The UAW leadership argued that these changes, which did not include a change in the rules of origin, ensure that the agreement will boost U.S. auto exports while protecting domestic production from Korean imports, thereby creating and protecting autoworker jobs.[70]

In reality, these concessions are unlikely to boost U.S. auto exports to Korea or help autoworkers.[71] One reason is that U.S. automakers tend to produce larger, more powerful cars than do Korean automakers. The market for these cars in Korea is relatively limited. Moreover, Japanese and European automakers already have a strong foothold in the "luxury" segment of the Korean market, and it is unlikely that the tariff reductions will prove substantial enough to help U.S. automakers gain significant market share.

An even more important reason is, as Jeffrey J. Schott notes, "U.S. automakers generally do not export many cars from U.S. plants beyond the neighborhood NAFTA market; instead, they produce abroad to supply foreign markets."[72] For example, GM's Korean subsidiary, GM Daewoo, currently produces approximately 900,000 cars annually in Korea. In 2008, more than 100,000 were sold to Korean customers, giving GM an 11.7 percent market share in Korea. By contrast, the combined Hyundai and Kia market share in the United States is only 7 percent, including the cars produced by Hyundai at its U.S. plant.[73]

Moreover, GM has far greater interest in other markets, especially China, where it is building market share through joint venture operations. GM operations in China now employ 32,000 hourly workers compared with 52,000 in the United States.[74]

The December 2010 changes also led Ford to endorse the KORUS FTA after first opposing it, although for different reasons than the UAW. The delay in tariff reductions will give Ford additional years of protection from Korean exports. Beyond that, Ford, like GM, has little interest in directly exporting to Korea from the United States. For the present, it continues to rely on its North American regional production and sales strategy. Its future plans for market expansion do involve Asia, but China, not Korea, is its main focus.

As Keith Naughton explained, Ford "remains barely competitive in China, with just 2.7 percent of the world's largest and fastest-growing auto market." Its weakness in this market is largely responsible for its overall declining global market share. In response, Ford aims to generate 70 percent of its growth over the next decade in Asia. To achieve this, it has embarked "on a building binge in Asia, spending $1.5 billion on new factories, including two assembly plants and an engine plant in China."[75] It is even possible that this new investment activity will eventually enable Ford to make inroads in the Korean market. In sum, it is difficult to see how the KORUS FTA will produce meaningful employment gains for U.S. autoworkers.

Tragically, the UAW's narrow focus on the job creation potential of tariff reductions led the union to largely ignore the destructive nature of the chapters that are also part of the agreement. This was a serious strategic mistake, since a key reason for the UAW's ever-weakening domestic position has been the U.S. auto industry's regionalization strategy, which received a major boost from the passage of NAFTA. Ironically, the Investment chapter contained in the KORUS FTA is modeled on the NAFTA Investment chapter.

In other words, the UAW treated the KORUS FTA as an honest effort to promote exports and jobs, rather than as a corporate effort to strengthen and expand existing economic processes. As a consequence, the UAW accepted an agreement that offers its members very little as it actually strengthens the regionalization dynamics that continue to marginalize the union. This decision will make it much harder for the UAW to organize against future agreements, or even existing corporate strategies.

At least in their public statements, most unions did, in contrast to the UAW, maintain a somewhat broader critique of the KORUS FTA, citing concerns about its various chapters (especially those dealing with government procurement and investment), as well as its lack of job-creating benefits.[76] For example, the International Association of Machinists (IAM) issued the following statement opposing the KORUS FTA:

> The current deal falls woefully short of addressing fundamental objections that have been repeatedly raised by the IAM. Among other things, the labor chapter fails to make any improvements on the inadequate Bush labor standards which were implemented in the Peru agreement over three years ago. It also preserves objectionable language regarding the investor to state dispute mechanism and contains troubling language concerning government procurement that could result in even more offshoring of U.S. jobs. . . .
>
> Not surprisingly, the same corporations that shipped thousands of U.S. jobs to other countries are now spinning Alice-in Wonderland tales about how this agreement will create jobs here at home. Given our past experience with NAFTA and other trade agreements and the current state of the U.S. economy, the nation can hardly afford to fall for this ruse again.[77]

This strong statement calls attention to the fact that the agreement offers numerous benefits to multinational corporations as opposed to workers. Yet at the same time little attempt was made to highlight the ways in which the terms of this agreement are little more than extensions of the same corporate dynamics and associated state policies that are undermining majority living and working conditions in the United States. For example, the Financial

Services chapter is simply a reflection of the growing dominance of financial services companies over U.S. economic activity. And the Government Procurement and Investment chapters are just extensions of the liberalization, deregulation, and privatization drive that is reshaping the role of the state.

Said differently, union critiques of the KORUS FTA tended to treat the agreement as a separate and distinct policy initiative, one that relates only to international processes and therefore can be considered and reformed in isolation from existing national economic and political dynamics. Unfortunately, treating the agreement this way has serious consequences. Most important, it encourages people to believe that if they can make the government aware of the agreement's shortcomings, it can and will correct them.

This belief was reinforced by most union leaders who routinely called the KORUS FTA the "Bush agreement" despite the fact that it was the Obama administration that ensured its ratification. The truth, which is easier to grasp once the terms of the agreement are understood as extensions of existing national dynamics, is that this agreement was not the result of ignorance or the desires of one political leader or party, but rather reflected a capitalist class project that is supported by the state for structural reasons, not partisan political ones.

The problematic nature of this approach is well illustrated by the 2010 "Joint Labor Declaration on the U.S.-Korea FTA," which Richard Trumka, president of the AFL-CIO, and Kim Young-Hoon, president of the Korean Confederation of Trade Unions, both signed. In the declaration, the two union presidents voice their opposition to the agreement because it "replicates many of the more troubling aspects of previous agreements, which privilege the rights of corporations over the rights of workers, consumers, and the general public." They state their concerns about "the potential impact of this agreement on employment and working conditions, particularly since both economies are struggling to emerge from the current economic crisis" and "the potential impact of the agreement on public and social services, the environment, and public health and education."[78]

The two leaders called for adoption of the Trade Reform, Accountability, Development and Employment Act of 2009, which they believe "contains important principles . . . [that] should guide the renegotiation of the KORUS FTA." The two leaders end their joint declaration by calling

> upon our governments to thoroughly review and renegotiate the KORUS FTA to ensure that it supports the creation of good jobs in both countries and to undertake the additional reforms needed to ensure that workers in both countries are afforded their fundamental labor rights, including their rights to organize and to bargain collectively. . . . If the trade agreement is not thoroughly reviewed and renegotiated to address our concerns we call upon elective representatives to oppose the KORUS FTA. In such a case, we will also call upon our members to vigorously oppose the KORUS FTA, in coordination with their unions and union federations.[79]

Unfortunately, the demand for "review and renegotiate" suggests that there is a basic core to the agreement that is acceptable. The implication is that contemporary capitalist accumulation dynamics provide an acceptable framework for structuring a fair, equitable, and responsive relationship between the two countries. The two leaders presented the agreement as likely to cause additional pain to workers who are already suffering from the consequences of a major crisis. But the agreement is more than just a policy initiative that will not encourage recovery. It is an extension of the very same policies that generated the economic crisis, the ones that promoted greater inequality and economic insecurity, the financialization of the U.S. economy, and the globalization of production. In fact, this agreement and others like it do more than just reinforce these policies; they actually establish them in law, making a future economic transformation more difficult to achieve.

The joint declaration concluded with a threat to defeat the agreement if needed changes are not made. But this stance left the movement vulnerable to governmental claims that minor modifications, such as the ones highlighted above dealing with the auto trade, represent a serious and satisfactory effort to improve the agreement. More to the point, the reality is that we cannot solve our economic problems by proposing an alternative trade policy, as if progressive trade policies could simply be soldered onto the existing political economy to form a new seamless, progressive whole. The logic of the existing political economy would make such a new policy impossible to implement or quickly corrupt it if it were somehow adopted.

This approach might be acceptable if it were aimed solely at influencing pubic officials while within the labor movement a more class-based, holistic organizing campaign was promoted. Unfortunately that is not what happened. The same perspective shaped internal organizing efforts, producing a movement with a limited political vision. As a consequence, even if the trade union movement had succeeded in defeating this agreement, it would be forced to start entirely new campaigns if it hoped to defeat other agreements waiting in the wings.

Although I have focused on the U.S. organizing experience, Korean activists faced their own specific challenges. The Korean movement built a strong opposition to the KORUS FTA. In 2006, over 300 social movement organizations, including trade unions, farmers' groups, and NGOs, formed the Korean Alliance against KORUS-FTA. Many demonstrations were organized against the negotiations and resistance intensified after the agreement was signed in April 2007.

Korean labor and social movement activists made a number of critiques of the agreement. However, they generally built popular support by framing the struggle against the KORUS FTA as one against U.S. efforts to colonize Korea. This was not a difficult argument to make. As noted above, the United States took advantage of its military-political leverage to force open the country to its drugs, cars, movies, and beef even before the start of negotiations. No doubt this framing made organizing easier, as it enabled opponents of the agreement to present themselves as defenders of Korean national sovereignty.[80]

As tempting as such a strategy was, there were many problems with it, problems that ultimately weaken the very movement that activists sought to build. For example, the focus on the threat of U.S. domination encouraged people to see the fight against the KORUS FTA as a national struggle between Korea and the United States. However, as discussed above, leading Korean corporations were enthusiastic supporters of the agreement. Since this nationalist orientation minimizes the importance of a class analysis, the fight against the KORUS FTA did little to build support for the broader struggle against the neoliberalization of the Korean economy and its destructive social consequences.

Perhaps more serious, this strategy encouraged participants in the anti–KORUS FTA struggle to believe that the agreement was dangerous only because it involved the United States. As a result, the movement was ill-equipped to build resistance to other agreements, including the Korean-European Union FTA (KOREU FTA). As the *Wall Street Journal* reported, EU ministers closely monitored "South Korea's free-trade talks with the United States to ensure that any new benefits given to the United States should also be granted to the EU."[81] Not surprisingly, then, Korea's agreement with the European Union closely resembled its agreement with the United States.

The European Union and Korea concluded an agreement in October 2010, and the European Union ratified the KOREU FTA in February 2011. Three months later the Korean parliament also ratified it, with strong support from Korea's leading corporations.[82] Having pursued a strategy that encouraged opposition to the KORUS FTA on the basis of resistance to U.S. domination, the Korean anti-FTA movement was unable to build significant opposition to the KOREU FTA. In fact, the Korean media promoted the desirability of the KOREU FTA by arguing that the European Union offers an alternative and in many ways superior form of capitalism to that of the United States.[83] The Korean government is also pursuing additional FTAs with Canada, Mexico, Australia, New Zealand, and Peru, and is in preliminary talks with China.

In sum, whether because of confusion about the relationship between FTAs and capitalist imperatives or for reasons of expediency, U.S. and Korean labor and social movements generally embraced anti–KORUS FTA strategies that treated the agreement as a mistaken national policy initiative. In the case of the United States, this meant that the anti–KORUS FTA movement largely reinforced, rather than transformed, working-class beliefs that free trade is a desirable goal, the U.S. government is a class-neutral defender of the national interest, free trade agreements are complex technical documents that must be evaluated on a case-by-case basis, and international agreements can be considered and understood separately from national dynamics. Therefore, despite the hard work of many activists, the movement never succeeded in building a significant popular challenge to the ratification of the KORUS FTA.

As we have seen, FTAs have become an essential part of the capitalist effort to establish a global infrastructure suitable to its contemporary accumulation dynamics. This perspective helps to explain why leading corporations from different countries have been eager to encourage their respective governments to negotiate them and why governments have embraced the task.

There is no question that these agreements should be opposed. However, treating each agreement as a separate initiative that needs to be defeated because it is destructive of working-class interests is a recipe for exhaustion and failure. Like the mythical Hydra, capitalism is fully capable of generating agreement after agreement.

The challenge is to develop a successful strategy. Here we can draw upon the example of Heracles and Iolaus: we should oppose each agreement in a way that promotes clarity about its origins and aims, and then build upon the gains from each separate struggle to shape and advance a popular movement to transform capitalism itself. It is not too late to tap in to the anger, insights, and solidarity created and nurtured by anti–KORUS FTA activists on both sides of the Pacific to make a giant step forward.

4—After Seattle: Strategic Thinking about Movement Building

There was a time, not that long ago, when growing numbers of people eagerly embraced an anti-neoliberal globalization perspective. Perhaps the high point of that period was the huge mobilization that helped to disrupt the 1999 WTO ministerial meeting in Seattle, Washington. The WTO process never regained its momentum despite repeated attempts by developed capitalist governments to launch new rounds of negotiations.

This chapter is based on an article I wrote shortly after the "Battle in Seattle." Both the organizing and energy that predated the Seattle actions as well as the new alliances and coalitions that resulted suggested great promise for building an internationally connected movement capable of challenging capitalist imperatives.

Unfortunately, the anti-globalization movement eventually weakened and then dissolved, due in no small part to the U.S. government's successful militarization of domestic and foreign policy following the 2001 attack on the World Trade Center. Now, Occupy Wall Street and the movement it spawned serve as the reference point for possibilities in the United States. Despite the

*fact that contemporary economic, political, and social conditions
are different from what they were at the end of the twentieth century, the two movements share many similarities, and activists
today face many of the same challenges that confronted anti-
globalization organizers, including how best to shape demands,
build campaigns, and advance movement building. In short,
strategy remains a major consideration.*

*Because this article was first and foremost concerned with
strategy, I believe it remains timely. In particular, the issues
addressed remain critical to our ability to successfully confront
capitalist globalization, including how to relate to China's role in
the global economy, respond to deteriorating labor conditions in
the United States and abroad, enhance international solidarity,
and create transformative social movements. As a result, I have
included it in this book largely unchanged.*

The Seattle anti–World Trade Organization actions have justifiably
generated a lot of excitement, renewed political activism, and produced considerable serious discussion on the left about next steps.
For the first time in a long time, we are in the position to think
and act strategically, with movement building in mind. In what
follows, I evaluate the Seattle experience; examine several political
initiatives; explore the relationships among issues, campaigns, and
movements; and suggest political criteria and a program of action
to guide our organizing efforts. My aim is to help achieve the political clarity and unity necessary to realize the potential of the period.

Celebrating Seattle

The Seattle actions were noteworthy for their inclusiveness and
creativity, as people of many different ages, motivated by many
different concerns, joined together in opposition to the WTO
and the neoliberal policies that define its agenda. Those directly

involved in the demonstrations withstood attacks by the police and National Guard with incredible spirit, determination, and solidarity. Demonstrators have done an excellent job carrying the message of those days back to their communities, often to large and enthusiastic audiences. Many have published useful summaries and critical analyses of the events.[1]

As we celebrate the battles won on the streets of Seattle, it is important that we not lose sight of the broader social developments that give the Seattle events even greater political significance. The following are among the most important: a substantial and growing number of working people are angry that their working and living conditions have shown little (if any) improvement during this period of economic expansion. In addition, many are coming to understand that this situation is not the result of a natural, evolutionary process (often called globalization), but rather of conscious choices that reflect political interests defined primarily in terms of capitalist imperatives. And many are also beginning to realize that working people throughout the world face similar trends and political processes, and that joint action is not only possible but necessary if positive changes in living and working conditions are to be achieved.

The overwhelming majority of people who participated in and supported the Seattle demonstrations would not define themselves as radicals, but their understandings and motivations demonstrate receptivity to a radical understanding of capitalism and socialist-oriented political action. The post-Seattle period thus represents an important and exciting opportunity for those of us committed to building strong and democratic movements for socialism.

At the same time, there is nothing automatic about the future direction of political developments. Most of the teach-ins, both before and after the WTO protests, offered an array of political perspectives, from anti-corporate to anti-consumerist to anti-capitalist. Some presenters advocated elimination of the WTO; others called for its reform through the incorporation of labor and environmental side agreements. Calls for defensive struggles to protect labor rights or the environment often mingled uneasily with calls for new forms of living and working in intentional, self-sufficient communities.

Therefore, this period requires—if not demands—that we think carefully about how to respond to the anger and energy people are feeling and expressing. In other words, we need to develop a strategic focus that can help us build movements for change that embrace the principles of equality, democracy, and solidarity in both practice and vision. Lacking such a focus, it is all too likely we will miss a highly favorable moment for making real progress toward socialism. However, urgency does not always bring clarity.

A Flawed Strategy: The China Campaign

Concern over deteriorating labor and environmental conditions motivated many working people to oppose the WTO. President Clinton, recognizing the seriousness of this concern, sought to blunt its radical potential by acknowledging it and advocating adoption of a labor study group as a first step toward the incorporation of labor standards into the WTO. A number of activists and groups involved in the Seattle actions proposed a different response to this concern, one that they hoped would strengthen ties between labor and other social groups and popular opposition to the WTO. Their strategy was to direct popular energy into a campaign opposing China's entry into the WTO. Unfortunately, this is a seriously flawed strategy. Such a campaign misdirects the political energy of the period. It is unlikely to deepen an understanding of the nature of capitalism or build a socialist-oriented movement for change.

Shortly before the Seattle meetings, the U.S. and Chinese governments agreed on terms under which the United States would approve China's entrance into the WTO. These terms said nothing about labor rights or environmental standards. However, for the agreement to have force, the U.S. Congress must first vote to grant China permanent Normal Trade Relations (NTR).

Groups such as *Public Citizen* and leaders of the AFL-CIO oppose the China deal for a number of related reasons. They consider China to be a "world-class" dictatorship, unfair trader, and exploiter of working people. They believe that China's entrance into the WTO will intensify downward pressures on working and environmental conditions in the United States and elsewhere. In sum, they find the China deal to be symbolic of all that is wrong with current globalization dynamics, and they are convinced that they can use the momentum from Seattle, as well as public distrust of China, to win the vote against NTR for China and strike another blow against those that support unregulated international capitalism.

Recognizing the potential significance of the China-NTR debate, the *Wall Street Journal*, in a front-page story titled "WTO's Failure in Bid to Launch Trade Talks Emboldens Protestors," offered a profile of leading progressive voices in the movement to keep China out of the WTO:

> The [WTO] talks' collapse left foes of free trade euphoric. And they left Seattle with a new energy, intent on fighting the Clinton administration's next major trade goal: getting China in the WTO. "China. We're coming atcha," yelled Mike Dolan, master planner of the Seattle protests, as he celebrated the disintegration of the WTO ministerial meeting. "There's no question about it. The next issue is China."[2]

The article quotes a number of people associated with the AFL-CIO making similar statements. AFL-CIO spokeswoman Denise Mitchell said, "The China vote is going to become a proxy for all of our concerns about globalization." The article also highlights the position of Jeff Faux, president of the progressive Economic Policy Institute (EPI), who opposed China's entrance into the WTO because its presence would make it "impossible to get labor and environmental standards." The reason is that China is not only a dictatorship, it is also too big a country to push around.

This strategy of making the China issue our main issue is problematic for several reasons. Most important, it encourages people concerned about labor and environmental conditions in the United States to see China as largely responsible for these conditions, not U.S. capitalists or capitalism in general. This leads people to think that the best response to U.S. problems is to force China to change its system, perhaps by adopting U.S.-shaped labor and environmental regulations, and by extension, that there is nothing fundamentally wrong with U.S. capitalism.[3]

These are not abstract fears. A case in point is an article by Robert E. Scott, an EPI economist, which was published in the progressive journal *WorkingUSA*.[4] Scott opposes China's entry into the WTO for several reasons, the most important of which is that its statist system does not allow for fair trade. Thus admittance into the WTO will result in increased trade problems for the U.S. economy.

Scott proposes three conditions that, if met, would allow him to end his opposition:

> First, the United States should oppose China's WTO membership unless and until China agrees to include enforceable labor rights and environmental standards as core elements of the agreement. Second, the United States should not enter into any trade agreement with China that does not deliver quantifiable commercial benefits. . . . [This requires China to] agree to maintain or appreciate the value of its currency as needed . . . [and] agree to achieve quantifiable, numerical targets for import penetration at the product and industry level, under strict timetables. Finally, all of these agreements must be enforceable through a clearly defined multilateral mechanism. Any changes required to make the WTO structure compatible with the necessary enforcement mechanisms would have to be put in place.[5]

There can be no mistaking the politics driving this article. Scott calls not for dismantling the WTO, but for strengthening it by

adding labor and environmental standards as well as new enforcement mechanisms for oversight of exchange rates and economic
activity in general.

What is it about China that excites such strong demands? Though
Scott states that China "exploits labor and represses human rights,"
his attack is primarily directed against the non-market features
of the Chinese system.[6] According to Scott, "Unfair competition
is built into China's economic system."[7] The reason is that China
uses "a number of market-distorting government policies, including requirements for technology transfer to domestic firms, local
content and offset requirements and import and foreign exchange
licensing arrangements."[8]

Significantly, when highlighting the growing U.S. trade deficit
with China in key sectors such as computers and telecommunication equipment, Scott points out that China's high-tech exports to
the United States are produced largely by U.S. and other foreign
multinationals operating in China. He says, for example, "As in
the case of computers, the United States exports parts and jobs to
China's 'export platforms' (foreign-owned factories within China
that import parts and export finished goods), and it gets assembled phones in return."[9] Yet Scott raises no critical questions about
the destructive operation of U.S. multinational corporations or the
logic of export-led capitalism. His attacks are leveled only against
Chinese state policy, and in particular those parts of the Chinese
system that appear to deviate from neoliberalism.

No doubt many people mobilized by the events surrounding the
Seattle protests could be attracted to the campaign against China's
entrance into the WTO. The Chinese government is not democratic, and most Chinese workers labor under difficult and harsh
conditions. Moreover, there is little doubt that Chinese workers,
and especially farmers, will suffer greatly from their country's
entry into the WTO.

Still, it is important to realize that the campaign against the
China deal is not a solidarity campaign. Comparisons to boy-
cott actions against apartheid-era South Africa or to Burma are

revealing. In those cases, we had democratic forces within the country calling for trade and investment boycotts as part of their own internal strategy for achieving change.

To date, no independent movement of Chinese workers has called for international support for a campaign to keep China out of the WTO. In fact, even organizations operating in Hong Kong that seek to promote independent labor organizing in China have refrained from supporting such a campaign.[10] Moreover, many militant and independent labor movements, including those in South Korea and Brazil, as well as many third world NGOs, have gone on record opposing the extension of WTO powers to include oversight of labor and environmental conditions. Thus pursuing a campaign that makes such demands a critical element of its strategy is bound to endanger the international solidarity that was built during the Seattle actions. This accomplishment should not be lightly cast aside.

The anti-China campaign makes sense only if the primary goal is reform of the WTO through adoption of labor and environmental side agreements. But such a goal not only undermines international solidarity, it sets back the political development of a socialist-oriented movement in the United States. A growing radicalization is taking place within the U.S. working class and our efforts should be directed toward deepening the process, not blunting it. A movement that calls for reform rather than rejection of the WTO, and that encourages workers to celebrate neoliberalism and pressure other countries to restructure their political economies along similar lines (so as to solve "our" problems) clearly leads in the wrong direction.

We should oppose making China the focal point of our political work. Our response to those who want to know our opinion on this issue should be that the Chinese people would be better off if their country remained outside the WTO, as would the working people of all countries, including those in the United States. That is why we oppose the WTO and seek to dismantle it. Fundamentally, the China-WTO issue represents a struggle among elites in both the

United States and China. Our attention and organizational efforts should be focused on developing campaigns that speak directly to workers' concerns in the United States and other countries, and that promote rather than weaken international worker solidarity.

An Alternative Campaign: Ratification of ILO Labor Conventions

There are other more productive ways to respond to the deterioration in U.S. working and living conditions that keep the focus on U.S. capitalism. One way is to take advantage of the U.S government's rhetoric. The president and most members of Congress, for example, claim to support strong labor rights. Yet their "actions" tend to be limited to criticisms of labor conditions in other countries. We should challenge the president to endorse, and the Congress to ratify, the seven fundamental labor Conventions of the International Labor Organization (ILO).

The ILO has adopted more than 180 international labor conventions. These conventions, in the words of the ILO, "are international treaties, subject to ratification by ILO member States." The ILO governing body has decided "that seven Conventions should be considered fundamental to the rights of human beings at work" and should be "implemented and ratified by all member States of the organization. These are called Fundamental ILO Conventions."[11]

These seven core labor standards are designed to protect freedom of association and organization (Conventions 87 and 98), abolish forced labor (Conventions 29 and 105), guarantee equality in employment and remuneration (Conventions 111 and 100), and eliminate child labor (Convention 138). At this time, the United States has ratified only one of these fundamental labor standards, number 105.[12] The ILO notes substantial divergence between U.S. national legislation and four of the fundamental conventions: 29, 87, 98, and 100.[13]

The International Confederation of Free Trade Unions (ICFTU) issued a report for the WTO General Council (as part of the latter's review of trade policies) that illuminates U.S. noncompliance with its international commitments.[14] The report notes, for example, that many U.S. workers are denied the right to join trade unions and bargain collectively. "In the public sector approximately 40 percent of all workers—nearly seven million people—are denied basic collective bargaining rights."[15] And in "the private sector, the law does not protect workers when the employer is determined to destroy or prevent union representation."[16] Examples cited include regular, unpunished firings of trade union activists and the use of permanent replacement workers during a strike. The report also notes that agricultural and domestic workers, as well as certain kinds of supervisory workers and "independent contractors," are not covered by the National Labor Relations Act.

The ICFTU report finds ongoing race and gender discrimination in the United States in both hiring and remuneration as well as the ongoing use of child labor, especially in agriculture and garment sweatshops. It also finds increased use of forced labor in prisons and in U.S. dependent territories, such as the U.S. commonwealth of the Northern Mariana Islands, where "imported" foreign workers are often forced to work under conditions resembling debt peonage.

The U.S. record of ratification of these fundamental labor standards is among the worst in the Organization for Economic Cooperation and Development (OECD) countries. A campaign to publicize this fact and demand ratification of all seven conventions has the potential to sharpen class-consciousness and deepen popular understanding of capitalist imperatives. Such a campaign could also promote greater international solidarity between U.S. and other workers. For example, conversations with workers in other countries could help the U.S. labor movement learn more about alternative legal frameworks and how they have influenced, and have been influenced by, labor organizing and workplace struggles.

A campaign to ratify the seven fundamental ILO Conventions represents only one possible alternative to the campaign to keep China out of the WTO. I have highlighted it to illustrate the choices we face and the importance of using well-formed political criteria to guide our political efforts. Other campaigns also deserve our support, including those that promote living-wage contracts, the transformation of the public sector, and opposition to sweatshop production and International Monetary Fund (IMF) and World Bank policies.

The Political Challenges of Campaign Organizing

Our challenges extend beyond developing sound political criteria and using them to determine which campaigns have the greatest progressive potential. We also face the challenge of working within our communities to share and win support for our political criteria and choices. For example, opposing the China campaign could lead to red-baiting or charges of sectarianism. More important, even when there is general agreement about which campaign to pursue, there is no guarantee that the campaign will realize its potential.

Campaigns are themselves complex political processes. There is no issue so "pure" that it guarantees that the associated campaign will promote grassroots participation; a class-conscious, anti-capitalist perspective; and international solidarity. There is always the danger that pressures from inside and outside the campaign will moderate the politics and narrow its focus, with disastrous political results.

For example, I have advocated a campaign for ratification of ILO core Conventions, seeing it as a vehicle for movement building. However, such a campaign, if dominated by reform elements, could easily fail to achieve this objective. Organizers could limit actions to postcard campaigns directed at members of Congress; people could be encouraged to see ratification of these conventions as the ultimate answer to U.S. labor problems. The outcome would certainly be a political dead-end. An examination of conditions in Germany and France, countries that have ratified all seven core Conventions, should make clear that ratification in and of itself has limited ability to challenge and transform capitalist dynamics. Even Guatemala ratified all seven.

Similarly, some anti-sweatshop campaigns come dangerously close to presenting sweatshops as a historical anomaly that can be ended by using consumer campaigns to encourage capitalists to change their behavior. As a result, many participants begin thinking in terms of good capitalists versus bad capitalists rather than developing an anti-capitalist consciousness. Even campaigns against the IMF and World Bank are divided along fix it-nix it lines, leading to competing political understandings and visions of change.

In short, campaigns can differ in terms of their organization dynamics and political focus even when addressing the same "issue." And, as is true with issues, some campaigns are more likely to promote favorable political outcomes than others. Therefore we must give careful attention to the choices we make when organizing campaigns if we are to succeed in building on the promise of this period. Happily, there are historical experiences that can help us develop criteria for, as well as suggest approaches to, successful campaign organizing.

Learning from History: The Example of May Day

An examination of the struggle for a shorter workday, which came to be symbolized by May Day demonstrations and strike actions, has much to teach us about how to organize around "reform" issues while simultaneously building militant, national, working-class movements and revolutionary visions. More specifically, the history offers important insights into how to maximize the radical potential of our campaigns and build meaningful international solidarity. It also highlights the critical nature of the relationship between campaigns and movements.

The struggle for a shorter workday in the United States began in the late eighteenth century, even before the establishment of the first trade unions. The goal was the ten-hour day. A key aspect of the campaign concerned the way organizers framed their demand. They argued that the ten-hour day was needed not only to protect the health of workers, but also because the long and exhausting workday was a barrier to more revolutionary change. A circular issued in 1835 by Boston workers advocating the ten-hour day highlights the connection: "We have been too long subjected to the odious, cruel, unjust and tyrannical system which compels the operative mechanic to exhaust his physical and mental powers. We have rights and duties to perform as American citizens and members of society, which forbid us to dispose of more than ten hours for a day's work."[17]

By 1866, although many workers still worked more than a ten-hour day, the labor movement had set its sights on achieving an eight-hour workday. Organizers continued to advance the demand for shorter hours as a necessary step in a longer process of social transformation, not as an end in and of itself. At its first convention in 1866, the National Labor Union declared, "The first and great necessity of the present to free the labor of this country from capitalist slavery is the passing of a law by which eight hours shall be the normal working day in all states of the American union."[18]

The International Workingmen's Association, also known as the First International, issued a similar statement, written by Karl Marx, two weeks later, which said: "The legal limitation of the working day is a preliminary condition without which all further attempts at improvements and emancipation of the working class must prove abortive. . . . The Congress proposes 8 hours as the legal limit of the working day." Noting the fact that workers in both Europe and the United States were demanding and striking for the eight-hour day, the resolution continued as follows: "As this limitation represents the general demand of the workers of the North

American United States, the Congress transforms this demand into the general platform of the Workers of the World."[19]

One argument used by employers against the demand for a shorter workday was that granting the eight-hour day would disadvantage them relative to employers in other countries. The effective response was to make the demand for a shorter workday an international demand, advanced by national labor movements as they saw best, in a manner that allowed each movement to support and gain support from the struggles of workers in other countries.

The Federation of Organized Trades and Labor Unions of the United States and Canada (precursor to the AFL, American Federation of Labor), which formed in 1881, quickly took up the demand for the eight-hour day. At its 1884 convention, it called for organized efforts to achieve the demand by May 1, 1886, when it planned to conduct massive strikes against employers who still resisted. There were indeed massive strikes that day.

These strikes provide the context for the May 4, 1886, Haymarket Square tragedy in Chicago. On that day, at the conclusion of a meeting called to protest police violence against striking workers, a large force of armed police entered the square and ordered the meeting to end. Before any action could be taken, a bomb was thrown into the audience. One of the police was killed instantly; many others were wounded. The police responded by firing at the assembled workers.

Business and government leaders, frightened by the growing strength of the labor movement, took advantage of the Haymarket incident. The police arrested eight working-class leaders and charged them with the murder of the policeman at Haymarket Square, despite the fact that most were not even present at the meeting. They were charged with encouraging the bombing through their speeches. All eight were found guilty in a rigged trial; four were hanged, one apparently committed suicide. The surviving three eventually were pardoned. The Haymarket Martyrs became the symbol for May Day.

Despite intense repression, the labor movement continued its eight-hour offensive. The AFL, at its 1888 convention, passed a resolution targeting May 1, 1890, as the date for labor to take massive strike action to achieve its goal. Educational and organizational campaigns, including demonstrations, were scheduled to take place in the intervening period.

As in 1866, the U.S. call to action was taken up by the international workers' movement. The Second International was founded in France in 1898. Samuel Gompers, president of the AFL, sent a communication to its meeting in Paris, informing those present of the AFL's strike strategy and asking for their support. A French delegate was preparing to offer a resolution calling for coordinated international actions by workers to win the eight-hour day. In recognition of the U.S. request, he selected May 1, 1890, as the designated day.

Unable to organize a general strike for May 1, the AFL eventually decided on a strategy that called for one group of workers to spearhead the struggle. In 1890, it was the carpenters. Other workers were to strike if they could, but all workers were encouraged to demonstrate their support for the demand. Workers continued to view the eight-hour day as a step in a larger struggle against capitalism. This understanding is captured by the slogan that New York demonstrators displayed on a banner at their meeting: "NO MORE BOSSES—WAGE SLAVERY MUST GO AND THE 8-HOUR DAY IS THE NEXT STEP IN THE LABOR MOVEMENT. THE SOCIALIST COMMONWEALTH IS THE FINAL AIM."[20]

There were more strikes on May 1, 1890, than on any previous day in U.S. history. That day also proved to be an international day of action by workers. Strikes and demonstrations took place in most of the world's main industrial cities. The initial resolution of the Second International calling for action on May 1, 1890, was not intended to establish a May Day tradition. But the success of the day encouraged labor movements throughout the world to maintain that day as their day of collective struggle; May Day thus became international workers' day.

In the struggle for the eight-hour day, as in all struggles that are framed to engender vast social change, political differences developed over time. In many countries, the official trade union movement began seeking ways to undermine the radical significance of the day. Some began organizing May Day celebrations on the closest Sunday so that they would not have to organize strike actions. By the early 1900s, the AFL was even denying that it had any role in the origins of May Day and actively opposed strikes on that day.

The Second International fought mightily against this trend, officially calling on workers' movements to maintain actions on May Day and, to the greatest degree possible, engage in strikes and organize events that deepened the class understanding and class character of the struggle. But over time victories as much as defeats—and even more so repression—gradually weakened the movements and traditions that kept alive the revolutionary spirit of May Day. The U.S. government sought to portray May Day as a holiday of foreign inspiration by promoting its own official labor day. Making clear what was at stake, in 1955 the U.S. government declared May 1 to be Loyalty Day.

Although capitalists and their supporters no longer fear May Day, activists can still learn a number of important lessons from the history of the struggle for a shorter workday. Among the most important: specific demands for change should be placed in a broader, revolutionary context. Solidarity should be built by highlighting common national concerns and creating a framework for linking national struggles. And the success of campaigns ultimately depends on the strength of the movements that promote them.

Revitalizing the May Day Tradition

Beyond the value of its historical lessons, May Day remains important in its own right because it continues to offer a unique opportunity for rebuilding a radical movement.[21] First, considerable interest in the history of the day remains. This affords organizers a wonderful opportunity to reconnect working people in the United States with the country's history of labor militancy. Discussions of May Day history also provide a useful opportunity for activists to develop criteria for movement building as well as to learn how reformist trade union politics and government repression can weaken labor activism and solidarity.

The framework for organizing May Day activities can and should be maintained as well. As we have seen, May Day actions sought to combine encouragement for immediate struggles with promotion of a long-term struggle to transform society. In contemporary terms, May Day actions should encourage resistance to current injustices in the workplace and community. But they should also encourage a belief in and commitment to the development of a radically new society. Thus May Day organizing demands a serious effort to build community alliances.

One of the most exciting aspects of the anti-WTO effort was that it focused people's attention on capitalism and the need to overcome it. For example, individuals and movements engaged in social experiments involving new ways of living—whether through voluntary simplicity or the creation of intentional communities—were motivated to demonstrate against the WTO by the realization that their experiments could not be sustained as long as capitalism, with its drive to commodify every aspect of human existence, continued to prosper.

Their growing opposition to capitalism as a social system has created new possibilities for building labor-environmental alliances with a class perspective. By encouraging representatives from these and other key social movements to plan community-sponsored May Day events and actions jointly, activists can help deepen and broaden such alliances and, in the process, create a social framework within which resistance to the structures and organizational forms of capitalism can be combined with new visions of working and living.

The history of May Day also highlights the importance of the relationship between campaigns and movements. May Day actions were organized by worker-community movements, which were in turn strengthened by them. As these movements weakened, it became harder for activists to ensure that May Day actions retained their radical orientation. Eventually, the day itself lost its social significance. This is an important lesson because many contemporary activists, no doubt buoyed by the success in Seattle, have tended to focus almost exclusively on organizing new actions or campaigns. Although these activities are an important way to create connections and inspire future activism, they do not automatically lead to the development of movements capable of transforming capitalism. In other words, we must strive to ensure that our actions and campaigns are part of, and enrich, a broader movement-building strategy.

Building a Movement while Responding to People's Immediate Needs

Successful movement building involves creating strong, accountable, and politicized organizations; a community-based structure that connects these organizations; and a common commitment to struggle based on a shared vision of the future. At the same time, movements for social change must be responsive to people's immediate needs.

There are many ways activists can help build strong organizations within a community-based structure. First, we must take seriously the task of organization building. This means that campaigns and activities need to be organized in ways that encourage those who participate to join and become active in the organizations that speak to their concerns. It also means that organizations must take advantage of these actions to mobilize and engage their membership.

Second, we must ensure that organizations take internal education seriously. Many church, labor, environmental, student, and social justice groups have been successful at generating participation at events, but are far less successful in creating an internal space where members can discuss past actions, expand their political understandings, debate strategy, and participate in planning future actions.

Third, we must unite the many organizations into a community. One way is to create informal gatherings where activists from these organizations can share experiences and develop strategies that integrate the activities of their respective organizations into a common project.

All three tasks can and should be combined. For example, activist meetings should help promote greater understanding of, and respect for, the concerns of the various participants and the communities they represent. This understanding and respect should then be integrated into the internal education programs of the various organizations. In this way, people from different parts of the broader community can learn to appreciate the strengths and struggles of others. Solidarity is thereby built from the bottom up, not from the top down. This solidarity makes it easier for organizations to plan common events and actions and to secure broad-based participation from their respective memberships.

Successful movement building also requires the development of a shared vision of the future. This, in turn, requires the development of a clear and well-focused political program of action. Ultimately, it is through political action that trust is built, community is formed, and new possibilities for living and working are imagined and created. If socialism is to provide the framework for achieving human liberation, it must be based on principles of equality, democracy, and solidarity. Therefore these principles must guide the development of our political program and the proposed actions must in turn give these principles concrete meaning and strengthen people's commitments to them.

A program of action must also respond to people's immediate needs. Since capitalism has left many working people struggling for survival, there is no shortage of needs to address. There are also many creative and increasingly successful efforts to improve conditions for working people in the United States and other countries. These include living wage struggles, anti-sweatshop struggles, and struggles directed at expanding and transforming the public sector. The first effort has already received a lot of publicity, so I will focus here on the second and third.[22]

Anti-Sweatshop Struggles

Anti-sweatshop struggles have considerable potential to advance the movement-building process. Beginning in the early 1990s, a number of groups began targeting apparel and footwear sellers such as the Gap and Nike for the brutal labor practices of their subcontractors operating in the third world.[23] The practices highlighted included child labor, unsafe and abusive working conditions, starvation wages, anti-union repression, and intolerably long hours. Anti-sweatshop activists built coalitions with unions, community and human rights groups, and third world NGOs, and organized demonstrations and consumer boycotts to demand economic justice for third world workers.

The efforts of these activists succeeded in bringing visibility to the human dimension of an increasingly complex global structure of production and encouraging consumers to think of their purchasing decisions in more political terms. Demands for change eventually grew strong enough that companies were forced to respond.

The corporate response has so far been limited, however. Some companies have instituted codes of conduct that have led to a decrease in child labor and improved safety conditions. Most have not. All companies continue to resist wage increases and unionization. In general, the leading firms in the apparel and footwear industries have focused their energies on trying to remove the issue from public view through use of the Fair Labor Association (FLA).

The FLA was established in 1998 as a result of meetings—convened by the White House—that included companies, unions, human rights, and religious groups. Despite its initial promise, the FLA clearly serves corporate interests. It does nothing to ensure livable wages or acceptable work hours; its monitoring system is corporate-controlled and limited in scope; and its enforcement mechanisms are almost nonexistent.[24] College and university students, who have reenergized the anti-sweatshop movement, have challenged this corporate attempt at obfuscation most forcefully.

Under the umbrella of the United Students against Sweatshops (USAS), students are demanding that school-licensed products be produced under conditions that are responsive to the needs of third world workers. This means that workers should be paid a country-specific living wage, have the right to unionize without fear of retaliation, and enjoy safe working conditions. Though a number of colleges and universities agreed to sign codes of conduct in line with these demands, no mechanism existed to secure corporate compliance. To overcome this problem, the USAS, with input from third world human rights and labor groups, developed its own monitoring organization, the Worker Rights Consortium (WRC). Students are now working to force their respective schools to withdraw from the FLA and join the WRC.

Fired up by the anti-WTO actions in Seattle, students have employed militant and highly spirited sit-ins and lockdowns at schools such as Johns Hopkins University, the University of Michigan, the University of Oregon, the University of Pennsylvania, and the University of Wisconsin. Some victories have been won. In February 2000, the University of Pennsylvania became the first school to withdraw from the FLA, followed shortly by the University of Wisconsin and Johns Hopkins. That same month, the University of Michigan, University of Indiana, and Oberlin College agreed to join the WRC.

Student activists also have worked hard to place their anti-sweatshop work in a broader political context. For example, the Student-Labor Action Committee at Johns Hopkins demanded not only that their university withdraw from the FLA and join the WRC, but also that it agree to pay a living wage to all who work at Johns Hopkins itself (including those employed by subcontractors), and create a shared committee to oversee school labor practices. By April 2000, victories include the university's withdrawal from the FTA and commitment to raise wages for the lowest-paid workers as well as report annually on its compensation policy. The students won strong support from community organizers, local high schools, unions, churches, and the city council. They still hope to make their school the first private-sector employer to adopt a living-wage agreement. This would be no small accomplishment. Johns Hopkins University and Health System is the largest private employer in Baltimore as well as Maryland as a whole.

The potential of these anti-sweatshop struggles lies in the fact that they encourage resistance to the corporate dominance of education, promote student-labor alliances, and strengthen international solidarity. They also draw new people into political movements for change.[25]

Public Sector Struggles

The struggle for social justice must be broadened, not only to include more people and to respond to more issues but also to directly challenge capitalist institutions and imperatives on both an ideological and material level. One way is to develop new organizing campaigns around the expansion and reconceptualization of the public sector. The ideological struggle over the public sector is of immense importance to the future of socialism. For historical reasons, most working people cannot conceptualize alternatives to a world anchored in private property. As Daniel Singer explains:

> The ideology of private property is triumphant today neither because people are especially fond of it nor even because the propaganda in its favor is so overwhelming. The campaign is

successful because of a void, because of the Soviet bankruptcy and the social-democratic failure. Why fight for something else when it turns out that it is either roughly the same thing with another label or a different, though no lesser, form of exploitation? For social property to be attractive once again, it will have to be perceived as the means to an end, as an instrument enabling the "associated producers" to gain mastery over their work, over their social environment, and thus, in a sense, over their fate.[26]

This fight to reclaim and revitalize notions of the public sector and social property must be waged on both national and local levels and as part of a long-term strategy. As a first step, we should organize in defense of public spending. Though living-wage and anti-sweatshop initiatives help reduce inequality and encourage commitment to the construction of a "society of equals," far more can and must be done through the public provision of essential goods and services, including quality health care, education, housing, and economic security. Therefore we must fight to ensure that adequate resources are progressively obtained and channeled into desired public programs. At the federal level, this means opposing the reduction or privatization of Social Security and supporting the use of the "budget surplus" to increase social spending.

Given our goal of social change, however, our strategy cannot be limited to the defense or even expansion of existing state programs. We must combine support for social spending with a strategy that encourages the transformation of the public sector. In other words, we must begin to make real the notion of social property. This strategy is best directed at state and local government activities and must be based on the creation of a shared political project that involves public-sector workers and labor and community groups.

Education may well provide the best starting point. The public education system in most cities and states is in crisis. Most teachers are underpaid and overworked and feel alienated from the larger community. School facilities are run down and budgets are tight. Moreover, hostile initiatives directed against the public school system and teachers win growing support from large numbers of private-sector workers. One example of this is the use of standardized tests to shape the curriculum and monitor teacher and school performance.

Working people are victims of these trends. Perhaps the biggest losers are children from working-class families who end up receiving an increasingly narrow and low-quality education. And, of course, belief in the public sector is another casualty.

One response to this situation is to facilitate meetings between public school teachers sympathetic to radical change and activists from different communities who share a common political commitment. The WTO experience has already helped to identify some participants. The meetings should have a one-item agenda: creating a responsive, engaging, and liberating system of public education.

Participants in the struggles against exploitation, imperialism, racism, sexism, homophobia, and environmental destruction understand that an educational system that helps young people develop appropriate values, skills, and commitments will enhance their efforts. Anti-WTO and anti-sweatshop actions have demonstrated that many students are eager to be involved in political struggle for a better world. Activists thus have every reason to work with politicized teachers and students to create space within the school system for a new, empowering curriculum that reflects and equips students to respond to current challenges. In other words, we must work to redefine the meaning of a public education.

The critical struggle for such a new education ultimately will take place within the school system, which means the leading voice in that struggle must be that of teachers. To this end, many public school teachers need opportunities to learn more about working-class history and social change and the interplay between these topics and pedagogy. Activist groups of teachers must increase their educational and organizing efforts among teachers while they simultaneously build links between the educational community and the broader activist community. One potential gain for teachers is increased community support in terms of dollars and respect. An even greater benefit is the ability to offer a meaningful educational experience to willing learners.

A political push organized in this fashion can create liberated spaces in the public education system and mobilize people outside of activist circles who care about what is happening to public education. Ideally, the process will slowly transform existing notions of public education. People will generate new expectations for "their" system, including that it function as a democratic and responsive arena for advancing new visions of society, with public school teachers serving as guardians of the public interest. Similar efforts can and should be launched around health care and social services of all kinds.

Though there are limits to how far such a process can develop within the existing capitalist system, the experience gained in the struggle should provide people with a greater appreciation of the benefits to be enjoyed when institutions are organized according to principles of equality, democracy, and solidarity as well as the desirability of having an economy based on social rather than private property. This is movement building that challenges capitalist rationality and puts working people in a position to shape their own social visions.

Of course, all organizing initiatives should be understood as parts of an integrated political strategy. For example, the movement to reshape public education requires the existence of a community of activists that are involved with, and accountable to, democratic and politically mobilized organizations. At the same time, it is only through efforts to win living-wage agreements, stop sweatshops, advocate for new labor laws, plan May Day activities, and remake the public sector that it is possible to create such a community.

In writing about political strategy, it is all too easy to move to the extremes. I hope I have avoided that trap. I do not want to minimize the obstacles to movement building or overstate them. Rather, my position is that we are in a period of possibilities.

Current economic, social, and environmental trends, as well as the initiatives and struggles highlighted above, strongly suggest that U.S. capitalism is ideologically vulnerable. And this is happening during the longest business cycle expansion in U.S. history; the next recession is bound to expand organizing opportunities greatly. Our challenge is to become better at learning from, and contributing to, ongoing mobilizations and struggles. If we succeed, our efforts may be rewarded by the creation of a movement powerful enough to offer a meaningful challenge to capitalist-inspired policies and practices. And if that movement enjoys relations of solidarity with movements elsewhere, the possibilities become truly exciting.

PART III

ALTERNATIVES TO CAPITALIST GLOBALIZATION

5—Learning from ALBA and the Bank of the South: Challenges and Possibilities

The early twenty-first century is marked by three overlapping developments: the failure of neoliberalism, the exhaustion of the East Asian export-led growth model, and Latin American efforts to advance an alternative regional development strategy. The combination has created a political environment offering important opportunities for those committed to the international struggle to supplant capitalism.

The failure of neoliberalism to deliver its promised growth has led to the creation of anti-neoliberal political movements throughout Latin America and Sub-Saharan Africa. Although a welcome development, their emancipatory potential has remained limited, in part, because many activists and intellectuals continue to draw a sharp distinction between neoliberalism and capitalism: they strongly oppose the former but remain unwilling to reject the latter.

Most tend to blame the development failures of their respective nations on government policies that liberalized, deregulated, and privatized economic activity. Many believe that the East Asian experience demonstrates that active state direction of economic activity can produce successful capitalist development. Thus they have often directed their efforts toward enhancing the capacities of their respective states in an attempt to re-create East Asian economic successes.

However, we are now at a point where it may be possible to win a majority of these activists and intellectuals to an anti-capitalist perspective, a critical change if we are to build the clarity and strength needed to advance a socialist alternative. One reason is that the exploitative nature of East Asian growth is becoming clearer. Another is that the region's export-led growth strategy finally appears to have run up against its own limits as structural weaknesses in the economies of the United States and Europe reduce the future demand for East Asian goods.

Perhaps most important, at the same time capitalism's credibility as an engine of development (in both free-market and state-directed forms) has been weakened, the governments of a number of Latin American countries are working to advance new regional initiatives that have the potential to promote and strengthen socialist-inspired development alternatives. The most significant are the Bolivarian Alliance for the Americas (ALBA) and the Bank of the South.[1] Although these two initiatives do not have the explicit mission of promoting socialist transformation, they are important because they concretize the existence of alternatives to capitalist growth strategies and, in the case of ALBA, offer support to governments that are pursuing a socialist-inspired process of transformation.

In what follows, I will highlight the failure of neoliberal policies and the shifting political orientation of many of the popular movements that oppose them. Then I consider, in some detail, the possibilities and challenges that ALBA and the Bank of the South present to those of us working to build a more egalitarian, democratic, and sustainable world. I conclude with six lessons drawn from this examination that can help increase the effectiveness of our efforts.

The Neoliberal Experience

Beginning in the late 1970s, advanced capitalist governments, led by the United States, sought to help their corporations gain greater access to third world markets. Among other things, they wanted third world governments to halt their efforts at import-substitution industrialization (ISI), which often involved state regulation of foreign trade and investment.

Their ability to impose their "free market" agenda on third world governments was greatly strengthened by the debt-triggered economic crises experienced by the majority of Latin American and Sub-Saharan African countries beginning in the early 1980s. By the end of the decade, over seventy countries were forced to accept International Monetary Fund (IMF) and World Bank structural adjustment programs requiring privatization, deregulation, and trade liberalization.[2]

The top concern for most third world governments during this period was to avoid defaulting on their international debts (most of which were incurred from past borrowings to finance ISI efforts and greatly increased by soaring international interest rates). This required pursuing policies designed to achieve a trade surplus. IMF and World Bank–mandated market openings made this task even harder by boosting imports (often leading to the bankruptcy of domestic firms). The result was the "lost decade," as governments were forced to suppress domestic consumption to generate the surpluses needed to meet debt obligations. Eventually, most found themselves forced to enter the competition to attract export-oriented transnational corporations, hoping that their investments would generate growth and the necessary export earnings for debt repayment.

The failure of these policies is easily demonstrated. For example, over the 1980s and 1990s, most Latin American and Sub-Saharan African countries continued to import more than they exported, resulting in ever-growing trade deficits that forced their respective governments to restrain growth.[3] The period was also marked by "reduced progress on social indicators for the vast majority of low- and middle-income countries."[4]

As a consequence, neoliberalism has been discredited among majorities in most Latin American and Sub-Saharan African countries, and popular movements in those countries are demanding a change in policies. However, most participants in these movements believe that development failures are best explained by the nature of state policies rather than capitalist dynamics. They are encouraged to do so because many movement activists and academics believe and argue that East Asia's growth record demonstrates that success under capitalism is possible if economic activity is shaped and directed by strong states rather than free markets.[5]

Unfortunately, this understanding of the East Asian experience is flawed. While activists and academics are right to stress the importance of state action, their desire to find a positive model of capitalist development led them to ignore the historically unique thus conditions that allowed the strong states of East Asia to form and encouraged core-country governments to (temporarily) support them. It also led them to overlook the high (and rising) political, social, and ecological costs underpinning East Asia's economic growth.[6] Finally, it led them to disregard the now obvious imbalances and contradictions generated by the region's export-dependent growth strategy.

There is reason to be hopeful that the struggle to overcome the limitations of anti-neoliberalism is gaining traction. One participant in the 2009 World Social Forum (WSF) in Belem, Brazil, highlighted developments as follows:

> In its first paragraph, the Declaration of the Social Movements Assembly stressed that "anti-imperialist, anti-racist, anti-capitalist, feminist, environmentalist and socialist alternatives are necessary to surpass the current crisis." This was the result of negotiations between two main groups: those in favor of neo-Keynesianism and those supporting a strong rupture with the bases of the different forms of the capitalist system. The

outcomes of the WSF clarified the debate: now there is a more explicit inclination by the composing organizations to support a rupture with the notions of economic progress, consumerism and commoditization of everyday life that have framed recent developments in capitalism.[7]

The cause of this shift in majority opinion is not yet clear. Perhaps it is due to greater clarity about the nature of the East Asian experience (thanks in part to the work of various international social forums like the WSF). Perhaps it is due to the ways in which the worldwide economic crisis that began in 2008 has revealed the problematic nature of capitalist accumulation dynamics. Perhaps it has been encouraged by recent Latin American efforts to advance a socialist-inspired development alternative, efforts that have likely stimulated critical thinking about the social and environmental aims and consequences of development itself.

What is clear is that this change in political perspective could prove temporary. For example, if economic conditions remain depressed, activists might once again be encouraged to embrace a more reformist agenda, viewing it as the most effective way to help working-class majorities obtain relief. We must continue to take this ideological struggle within the international progressive community seriously.

What makes this a most auspicious historical moment for supporters of socialism is that while capitalism is rocked by economic crisis, several Latin American governments are involved in advancing two new regional institutions with the potential to promote an alternative process of development: ALBA and the Bank of the South. Three of these governments—Cuba, Venezuela, and Bolivia—explicitly support the construction of socialism (although defined and pursued differently). This is a critical development, since isolated national efforts to build socialism are unlikely to succeed, especially when they are aggressively opposed by more advanced capitalist countries. That said, ALBA and the Bank of the South are not explicitly socialist vehicles.

ALBA

ALBA is the more far-reaching of the two Latin American initiatives. It was proposed by the Venezuelan government in 2001 as an alternative to the U.S.-promoted Free Trade Area of the Americas, and became operational in 2004, when Venezuela and Cuba signed the first ALBA exchange agreement. Seven other countries have since joined: Bolivia in 2006; Nicaragua in 2007; Dominica and Honduras in 2008; and Ecuador, St. Vincent and the Grenadines, and Antigua and Barbuda in 2009. Tragically, a U.S.-supported coup in Honduras installed a right-wing government, which withdrew the country from ALBA in 2010.[8]

ALBA is committed to a development strategy that is, in broad-brush, anchored by state-centered collaboration and designed to enhance the ability of participating governments to meet the needs of their working-class majorities. Its work is shaped by decisions made by a presidential council that are then formalized and implemented according to terms set by a ministerial council. ALBA's emphasis on state-directed activity was underscored by Venezuela's Vice Minister of Foreign Relations, Rodolfo Sanz, who declared that the key to ALBA's success will be the creation of "Grand-National Enterprises," by which he meant new regional public enterprises formed through agreements by national state enterprises as well as joint state collaborations based on partnerships between national state enterprises.[9] ALBA also has an advisory council of social movements that is supposed to provide direction to and oversight of the work of the other two councils.

In January 2008, ALBA countries created an ALBA Bank with capital of $1 billion.[10] In contrast to the IMF and World Bank, the Bank of ALBA does not impose loan conditions and functions on the basis of consensus. Its stated aim "is to boost industrial and agricultural production among its members, support social projects as well as multilateral cooperation agreements among its members, particularly in the field of energy."[11]

Underpinning ALBA's operation is recognition that each member nation, regardless of its level of development, has its own unique economic, social, and cultural strengths. ALBA thus provides a framework for governments to negotiate planned exchanges of the goods and services that reflect their respective nation's strengths. These exchanges allow each nation to pursue its own development objectives in a far more sustainable and equitable way than if forced to rely solely on its own resources or respond to global market imperatives.

Although still in its infancy, ALBA has already encouraged a number of important agreements and initiatives. For example, Venezuela provides Cuba with oil in exchange for the services of Cuban doctors and teachers. Venezuela and Cuba also have several joint agricultural projects involving the production of soybeans, rice, poultry, and dairy products. "Venezuela has also supplied Cuba with buses to improve its public transport system, assisted Cuba with the construction of a massive aqueduct to improve its water supply, and has helped Cuba revamp its main oil refinery."[12] The two countries have created a joint-venture transportation company, ALBA Transport, which has built two ships for transporting oil within the region. They are also pursuing the creation of jointly owned Cuban-based enterprises to produce stainless steel and nickel.

Venezuela and Cuba have several trade agreements with Bolivia. One of the most important involved the purchase of Bolivian soybeans after the United States signed a trade agreement with Colombia that resulted in a decline in U.S. demand for the Bolivian crop. Cuba is also helping Bolivia strengthen its education and health care systems. Cuba and Venezuela are also working with the Bolivian government to modernize and expand its natural gas industry. In return, Bolivia is providing natural gas and "mining, agriculture, agro-industrial, livestock and industrial products," as well as "knowledge on indigenous affairs and traditional medicine."[13] The governments of Venezuela and Bolivia are also planning new joint ventures for the production of steel, cement, and extraction of iron ore.

Dominica, too, has benefited from ALBA-organized cooperation. Cuba and Venezuela are helping modernize the country's
international airport and expand its oil storage and refining
capacities. Discussions are under way over terms of payment,
which are likely to involve return flows of Dominican goods and
services. Thousands of Dominicans have received free eye surgery
in Cuba, and Dominican youth are studying medicine at the Latin
American School of Medicine in Cuba.

Venezuela, Nicaragua, Ecuador, Bolivia, Honduras, and
Dominica have established a joint food production company with
the aim of securing food sovereignty for member nations. The
new "supranational" company will oversee a series of enterprises
that "will promote technological cooperation and training, invest
in rural infrastructure, and integrate regional food distribution."[14]
The project is being funded by a loan from the ALBA food security
fund managed by the ALBA Bank.

ALBA sponsors a number of important cultural initiatives.
For example, several member countries have established ALBA
Houses and are promoting exchanges between them. According
to Jose González, president of the ALBA House in Caracas, these
houses "will serve as centers for creativity, artists, cultural promot-
ers, social movements—to generate a movement that allows the
knowledge of values that at times are not recognized because the
mechanisms of the market are not interested in them."[15]

Although ALBA has so far failed to attract wide regional membership, it remains committed to its initial vision of a broader Latin
American process of integration and transformation through the
creation of "Grand-National Enterprises."[16] In doing so, it represents "the first attempt at regional integration that is not based
primarily on trade liberalization but on a new vision of social
welfare and equity."[17] The following is a partial list of the public
corporations that ALBA countries, in particular Venezuela, hope
to expand or create:

- TeleSur—a pan–Latin American television network financed by Venezuela, Cuba, Uruguay, and Brazil
- PetroSur—an association of state oil companies from Brazil, Argentina, and Venezuela for exploration, technological development, construction of refineries, and distribution
- PetroCaribe—a Venezuelan program to provide subsidized oil to fourteen Caribbean nations
- A Latin American and Caribbean airline
- The Insurance Company of the South
- A Latin American and Caribbean radio network

The global economic crisis has intensified ALBA efforts to move beyond its current emphasis on bilateral trade and investment agreements to promote a full-blown regional development process. In November 2008, member countries approved a decision to create an ALBA People's Trade Agreement with the goal of establishing an integrated economic and monetary zone with its own new currency, to be called the Sucre.[18] As negotiators continue to discuss operational principles for the zone, the Sucre is now being used in targeted trade, although only as a unit of account.

Several countries have deposited agreed-upon amounts of their respective national currency into a special Sucre bank. These funds were then revalued using the Sucre as the unit of account.[19] The first Sucre-denominated transaction, involving Venezuelan rice exports to Cuba, occurred in January 2010. Bolivia, Nicaragua, and Ecuador also have plans to engage in Sucre-denominated trade.[20] ALBA's long-term vision is for the Sucre to become an international reserve currency much like the euro.

ALBA's emphasis on public rather than private ownership, domestic rather than export orientation, social rather than profit motivation, and solidaristic rather than competitive relationships provides an important (ideological and material) counterweight to capitalist imperatives. It also represents an example of how states can create regional institutions that are capable of strengthening nationally centered development efforts. By providing a framework for state authorities to achieve popular goals through collective actions, ALBA ensures that gains in one country work to the benefit of others.

To this point, ALBA's promise remains greater than its achievements, although as highlighted above, these are not inconsequential. To some extent, this gap is understandable, given that the organization has been in existence for a relatively short time. Another reason is that few countries have joined, and most that have bring great needs and limited resources to contribute to the collective development effort.

At the same time, there are reasons for concern about ALBA's future. One is that ALBA remains heavily dependent on the decisions of the presidents of the participating countries. This means that actions are decided upon and implemented from the top down; at present, the social movement advisory council plays a very marginal role. This structure produces a bias toward large-scale mega-projects, many of which raise environmental concerns. Perhaps this will change. At the Ninth ALBA Summit, held in April 2010, ALBA presidents committed themselves to the organization of councils of social movements in each of their respective countries as a way of strengthening the ALBA council of social movements.

The top-down operation of ALBA also means that there is often no opportunity for popular discussion over how best to implement ALBA projects. This makes it harder to institute effective forms of worker participation in newly created public enterprises; ensure that educational, health, and media systems are responsive to the communities they serve; and establish planning mechanisms capable of directing social production in response to social needs. As a consequence, the transformative (socialist) potential of the overall ALBA effort is weakened.

A second concern relates to ALBA's heavy reliance on Venezuela. There can be no doubt that ALBA's progress to this point is largely due to the government of Venezuela's leadership and financial generosity. But there are also dangers (perhaps unavoidable) from the organization's dependence on one country.[21] One is that Venezuela could end up overwhelming and therefore undermining ALBA's decision-making process and organizational coherence.

Another is that too much weight could end up being placed on Venezuelan financial capacities. Many ALBA projects were initiated during the period of Venezuela's oil boom, when oil sold at almost $150 a barrel. Oil prices are now far lower, and there are indications that Venezuela may not be able to fulfill all its commitments. For example, Venezuela has fallen behind in its promised deliveries of oil to several Caribbean countries. Some oil and gas infrastructure projects are also being delayed.[22] For its part, Venezuela has publicly affirmed its commitment and ability to meet its obligations to the countries involved. Certainly, many important oil-related projects remain on schedule, including the construction of refineries in Manabi, Ecuador, and Cienfuegos, Cuba.

Such concerns suggest that the world economic crisis may represent a doubled-edged sword for ALBA. The collapse of world markets and currency instabilities give ALBA new legitimacy and add credibility to its call for the creation of new regionally based systems of planned trade and investment. At the same time, the resulting decline in oil prices threatens Venezuela's ability to sustain many of ALBA's existing programs.

Bank of the South

The Bank of the South is Latin America's other major effort to advance an alternative development process. Although the bank's stated agenda is more limited than that of ALBA, its potential to promote regional integration is in some ways greater because it includes most of the countries of South America.

The creation of the Bank of the South owes much to a common concern for regional independence by two different groups of South American countries: those led by governments that embrace a more radical project of social transformation (Venezuela, Bolivia, and

Ecuador) and those led by governments that are largely committed to a capitalist project but believe that success requires financial
independence from the United States (Brazil and Argentina). A
third group of countries, led by governments that continue to
embrace free-trade integration with the United States, has so far
rejected participation (Chile and Peru). Colombia, although also
close to the United States, has given mixed signals about its interest in membership.

Key to the bank's founding was the growing financial strength
of South American countries, fueled by the rapid post-2002 rise
in commodity prices (largely driven by demand from East Asia).
Supporters of the bank hoped that it would prove able to central-
ize "the savings of [member] countries, thus turning them into
productive investments and reducing the vulnerability of the
region to international economic cycles. This would be then laying
the foundations for a truly autonomous financial system, which
would contribute to the reduction of power asymmetries between
countries in the region, and would cut their dependence on international flows of capital."[23]

A February 2007 Venezuelan-Argentinean initiative launched
the process to create the Bank of the South; a formal proposal
followed one month later. Bolivia soon committed to the effort,
followed in relatively quick succession by Ecuador, Paraguay,
Brazil, and finally Uruguay. The bank was formally established on
December 9, 2007, and includes the seven countries as members.

The bank is still not operational, largely because the effort to
create it grew out of an alliance between countries that did not
share a similar political project. Intense debates and disagreements over a number of critical issues began immediately after the
start of negotiations. Among the most important: Would the bank
serve as both a monetary stabilization fund and development bank
or only the latter? Would decisions be made on the basis of one
country, one vote, or would voting power be based on the size of a
country's contribution (which would be based on economic size)?
Would the bank rely solely on member-nation contributions or

would it be free to raise money in international capital markets and from established international financial institutions that would participate as non-voting observers—with the latter two options dictating market-based lending rates and repayment terms?

Consensus was eventually reached on the most pressing issues, which made the bank's December 2007 establishment possible. The key points of agreement were as follows:

- The bank will operate solely as a development bank.
- The bank's headquarters will be in Caracas with regional branches in La Paz and Buenos Aires.
- Major decisions at the annual meetings of the bank's board of Directors will be made according to the principle of one country, one vote.
- Subscribed capital will be $7 billion; required capital contributions are $2 billion from Brazil, Argentina, and Venezuela, $400 million from Ecuador and Uruguay, and $100 million from Paraguay and Bolivia.

The seven presidents agreed that they would settle all remaining issues within sixty days. That deadline was not met. It was not until September 2009 that the seven presidents approved the bank's articles of agreement, which "contains rules that were negotiated by committees at the level of ministries of economy and finance, and include capital investments, a voting mechanism, recruitment of staff, case law, tax and legal considerations of officials and the functionality of the bank."[24]

Most important, it was decided that the bank will employ a hybrid voting model for credit decisions. Votes on loans of less than $70 million will be made according to the principle of one country, one vote; for loans over that amount, votes will be weighted in proportion to subscribed capital. It was also decided that the bank will make loans only to member countries for the execution of projects within South America. Finally, it was agreed that once operational, the bank could increase its capital to $20 billion.

Still undecided are questions about the bank's organizational structure (by department or areas of activity such as health or transport); the selection process for specialists (by country or expertise); the criteria to be used in selecting projects (countries, activities, need); interest rates and payment terms; the existence or absence of conditionality requirements; participation (limited to member nations or expanded to include non-voting observers such as international financial institutions); sources of funding (limited to subscribed capital or expanded to allow for international borrowing and/or contributions from observers).

The answers to these (and other) questions will go a long way toward shaping the bank's mission. The decisions will largely determine whether the bank's loans will be used to "finance large infrastructure projects which have huge socioeconomic impacts and meet the expansion needs of the main economic groups" or "favor the funding of solidarity projects aimed at the reduction of asymmetries in the living conditions of and among the different South American countries."[25]

To this point, differences between Brazil on one side and Venezuela and Ecuador on the other are the main reason for the bank's uncertain future. Brazil remains an unenthusiastic supporter of the bank; as the main regional economic power it is reluctant to accept limits on its ability to exploit that strength. Brazil has its own National Bank for Economic and Social Development, which in 2009 provided loans and lines of credit totaling more than $57 billion to support the domestic and international activities of Brazilian companies.[26]

Despite its opposition, Brazil apparently joined the Bank of the South because it feared remaining on the outside; inside, it had the ability to shape the workings of the institution. Brazil is strongly in favor of voting rights weighted by contributions and the use of market criteria in raising and loaning funds. Its vision of regionalization appears strongly influenced by the experience of the European Union; it wants to use the bank to encourage a regionalization process that will eliminate barriers to the free movement of capital, labor, and goods so as to help large national firms (most of which it expects to be Brazilian) become highly competitive multinational corporations.[27]

Despite Brazil's resistance to an alternative political project, the governments of Venezuela and Ecuador have been reluctant to push negotiations to the breaking point, fearing that Brazil might withdraw its membership. Because Brazil is the region's most important economy, they view its participation as critical to the bank's ability to achieve its goals. This situation has led to long and often inconclusive negotiations, leaving the bank's future in limbo. The Brazilian government may well be satisfied with this outcome.

Governments are not the only participants in this struggle over the bank's future. Latin American social movements were among the earliest supporters of the initiative and are actively engaged in efforts to force a conclusion to the talks on terms favorable to their more radical vision. In particular, they want strong criteria developed to ensure that the bank adopts an investment priority that supports, among other things,

> projects oriented toward food and energy sovereignty; the research and development of appropriate technologies for an endogenous and sustainable development of the region, including free software; the programmed and complementary production of generic medicines; the recovery of ancestral wisdom, systematized and accepted as an agroecologic science . . . and infrastructure that is based on different logics of spatial organization as implemented by local solidarity and self-managed development communities.[28]

In addition to national organizing, dozens of organizations from throughout Latin America have signed two different letters addressed to the presidents of the bank's seven member countries. Regional meetings have also been held to discuss strategy.

This interest and involvement in the struggle over the future of the bank stands in sharp contrast to Latin American civil society's lack of engagement with ALBA. As two researchers commented, "Consciousness of ALBA is not yet particularly high within the region's social movements and political leadership. There are very few serious analytical documents on the topic and even fewer that present concrete proposals from civil society groups for the process."[29] This is puzzling and disappointing. One possible explanation is that the bank includes more countries, in particular Brazil and Argentina, both of which have active, regionally linked social movements. Another is that many social movement activists view ALBA as a state-dominated institution, and they remain distrustful of states.

Unfortunately, the global financial crisis that began in 2007 also threatens the promise of the Bank of the South. The resulting decline in world trade and investment has created financial problems for a number of Latin American countries, including some that are members of the Bank of the South. In response, the major international financial institutions (hoping to reestablish their influence), quickly established new lending facilities specifically targeted for the region. Though Bank of the South member countries have so far rejected any new dealings with the IMF, several have sought and received significant new loans from the Inter-American Development Bank and other multilateral financial institutions, such as the World Bank.

If the Bank of the South had been operational before the start of the crisis, it is possible that it could have helped its member countries better withstand the crisis and avoid renewed pressures to adopt neoliberal policies. At the Mercosur Summit in January 2009, Ecuador's President Correa "spoke of the failure of the Bank of the South to help buffer the negative effects of the global economic crisis as a major issue, noting that, if it were more consolidated, its funds would have 'coordinated savings' and generated resources to compensate for the loss of foreign investments in the region. [Venezuela's President] Chávez has also reportedly commented that Banco del Sur will remain 'on ice' for the moment."[30]

Six Lessons

The fight to supplant capitalism will not end soon. But there is reason to believe that we are living in a time not only of great challenges but also of great possibilities. How should we respond? I offer the following six lessons, drawn from the above work, as guideposts for future political activity.

First, we must redouble our efforts to shift the political weight within progressive communities from anti-neoliberal to anti-capitalist. One way is to guard against uncritically promoting the anti-neoliberal critiques of liberal mainstream economists, such as Paul Krugman, Joseph Stiglitz, and Jeffrey Sachs, as if they were our own. Another is to deepen our own theoretical understandings of capitalism to better establish that neoliberalism is not simply a set of policy tools that governments are free to use or discard; rather, it represents the historically specific form that capitalism takes in certain regions and at certain times. We also need to deepen and strengthen our critical analysis of the East Asian experience so as to discredit the false belief in the potential of (state) capitalism to serve majority needs.

Second, we should maintain a cautiously supportive stance toward regionalization. Although Lain American social movements have good reason to support initiatives designed to promote it, struggles within the Bank of the South highlight the fact that regionalization has a contested meaning. We need to pay careful attention to what its proponents declare to be its aims and critically examine whatever processes are proposed to achieve it.[31]

Third, we must take state power seriously. Despite the beliefs of many social movement activists that structural transformation will best be achieved through grassroots, cross-border efforts, the most promising gains continue to be made by states, whose actions are largely a response to distinctive national political processes (most of which remain disconnected from world and regional social forum discussions and initiatives). ALBA is a case in point. It remains the most promising effort to promote an alternative development process, and its structure and policies are largely shaped by the policies of three nations (Venezuela, Cuba, and Bolivia), each of which is led by a government that proclaims its commitment to the building of a socialist-oriented political economy.

The Bank of the South represents a different project. It enjoys strong social movement support because those movements believe that it can eventually become powerful enough to "force" states to adopt policies that strengthen an alternative regional development process. However, the bank remains nonfunctional precisely because dominant states oppose this outcome, and it appears doubtful that these states can or will be forced to change their political orientation because of regional grassroots pressure. In short, national struggles and state power remain critical to achieving change.

Fourth, it appears that the most appropriate regional structures (at least for the present period) are those that have the fewest binding constraints on participating countries. Again ALBA and the Bank of the South provide an instructive contrast. ALBA does not exist as an "independent" institution with its own vision of, or mandate to, advance socialism (however defined). In fact, it includes member nations led by governments that are not pursuing this goal. These governments participate because they believe that their respective populations (or perhaps their political legitimacy) will benefit from the terms and forms of the negotiated collaboration.

ALBA is not hobbled by the same constraints as the Bank of the South because its structures are designed to afford participating governments maximum flexibility, thereby supporting those nations desiring a faster and deeper social transformation without forcing that transformation on less radically inclined ones. If socialist alternatives to capitalism are to develop and prosper, it will be because of the outcome of ongoing political struggles in those nations already committed to this goal, with the shared processes promoted by ALBA providing invaluable material and political assistance.

Fifth, state power alone is unlikely to produce the transformation in social relations required for a meaningful advance toward socialism. Latin American social movements are right to be wary of a state-directed process of change. Because the ALBA project is state-driven, there is reason for concern that the transformations encouraged in most member nations will be more bureaucratically than popularly oriented. ALBA collaboration can help strengthen state control and direction of the economies of member nations, but there is no guarantee that the resulting state planning and production will be structured to ensure meaningful worker and community participation in relevant decision making.

Building strong, democratic, and collaborative worker-community organizations and structures of planning is no simple matter. But there is a wealth of experience to be found in the cross-national discussions and collaborations that are nurtured at world and regional social forums and in the organizing work they generate and support. We need to find ways to strengthen these efforts and integrate the lessons learned into the processes of national change that are under way in the countries most committed to building socialism. This is a large challenge, but one we must surmount if we are to make meaningful progress in building alternatives to capitalism.

Finally, we must develop a more nuanced understanding of the consequences of capitalist crises. It is easy to believe that a structural capitalist crisis such as the one we are currently experiencing will automatically strengthen our efforts to replace capitalism. However, although the crisis is indeed delegitimizing capitalism as an engine of "progress," the weakening global economy is greatly complicating, if not weakening, efforts to advance ALBA as well as the Bank of the South.

We cannot simply rely on capitalism's contradictions to do the work of building support for a socialist alternative. No country is immune from the consequences of the crisis. That makes it even more important that we commit to deepen our educational work—work that makes clear that socialism represents more than a promise to produce more goods and services than capitalism. Socialism represents the possibility of a new way to live and work that brings with it a deeper satisfaction, in large part because of its ability to shape more mutually rewarding and sustainable human connections.

6—ALBA and the Promise of Cooperative Development

Existing international economic institutions and relations operate in ways detrimental to third world development. That is why eight Latin American and Caribbean countries—led by Venezuela, Cuba, and Bolivia—are working to build the Bolivarian Alliance for the Americas (ALBA), a regional initiative designed to promote new, non-market structures and patterns of economic cooperation.[1]

ALBA does this, in part, by providing a framework for member governments to create partnerships between existing national state enterprises as well as new regional public enterprises. The resulting initiatives, although still few in number, have helped member governments strengthen planning capacities, modernize national industrial and agricultural operations, and provide essential social services to their citizens.

In response to worsening international economic conditions, ALBA stepped up efforts to promote a full-blown regional development process. In November 2008, member governments announced their support for an ALBA People's Trade Agreement that "protects our countries from the depredation of transnational capital, foments the development of our economies and constitutes a space liberated from the inoperative global financial institutions and the monopoly of the dollar as the currency for trade and reserves."[2] Although the precise terms of the agreement are still being negotiated, official statements point to the creation of an integrated trade and monetary zone, with a new regional currency, the Sucre.[3]

This is a bold initiative that deserves to be taken seriously. Doing so requires grappling with some critical questions. How important or necessary is this initiative? How should the zone be structured? What are the potential challenges to, and benefits from, a successful outcome? These are big questions and, given that ALBA has not yet concretized its own plans, difficult to engage in a productive way.[4]

However, we do have the benefit of history; this is not the first attempt at collective regional development. One of the most successful attempts, and perhaps the most relevant for understanding and evaluating ALBA's effort, took place in Europe shortly after the end of the Second World War, when members of the Marshall Plan–sponsored Organization for European Economic Cooperation (OEEC) established the European Payments Union (EPU).[5] Studying the EPU experience offers us a practical way to begin thinking about these questions and the promise of cooperative development.

In what follows, I first discuss the rationale for a cooperative development strategy. Next, I analyze the political-economic dynamics that led powerful European countries to commit to such a strategy. Then, I examine the workings of the EPU as well as the dynamics leading to its eventual dissolution. I conclude with a discussion of relevant lessons for ALBA countries.

The Need for a Cooperative Development Strategy

Third world countries face enormous obstacles to development, of which the majority are the consequence of forced integration into the capitalist world system. One of the most difficult obstacles to overcome is a historically created import dependence. Weak and distorted industrial and technological sectors (and, in many cases, limited agricultural and primary commodity production capabilities) mean that third world attempts to boost economic activity normally trigger, at least in the short run, a sharp rise in the demand for imports.

If third world countries remain open to global market forces, their governments must find ways to obtain the foreign exchange necessary to finance the import surge. This means that most third world governments are forced, almost from the beginning of their development effort, to give priority to the creation of a competitive export sector, which involves channeling resources into satisfying foreign rather than domestic needs.

The complications quickly multiply. One of the fastest ways to establish a competitive export sector is to attract export-oriented transnational corporations. Unfortunately, because third world countries face similar development challenges, their governments end up competing to attract the desired foreign investment, offering ever greater labor, tax, and environmental concessions.

Growth is possible under such conditions, at least for a few countries. However, given the nature of transnational production networks, even the "successful" ones find it difficult to use their gains from trade to promote a domestically responsive and self-reinforcing process of technological and social development.

Aware of the destructive consequences of global market dynamics, some third world governments have tried to de-link their respective economies from the capitalist world system. However, this too has generally proven an unworkable strategy. Among the most important reasons is that few governments have the organizational capacity, much less the power, to refashion or reorient sufficient economic activity to achieve significant de-linking. Another reason is that few countries have the resources required to meet national needs without substantial trade.

Not surprisingly, then, there is need for an alternative development strategy. It is in this context that we can best appreciate

ALBA's interest in collective development, as expressed by the goals of its People's Trade Agreement. In brief, this approach represents a "middle-ground" strategy of group de-linking. ALBA governments hope that de-linking will provide the protection they need to engage in the coordinated planning and production required to overcome existing economic distortions and weaknesses. And, by acting as a group, these governments hope to ensure that their respective national enterprises will have access to the broader markets they need to enjoy economies of scale and obtain scarce resources and technology.

ALBA's effort is, in many ways, unprecedented, especially because ALBA is composed of countries with diverse political visions; for example, three—Bolivia, Cuba, and Venezuela—are led by governments explicitly committed to building socialism. Still, there have been other attempts at cooperative development that can help shed light on the challenges and choices facing ALBA. This is true even if they were organized by capitalist governments to further capitalist interests.

When capitalist governments are under great pressure—as they were in the 1930s when the Great Depression forced them to initiate a series of public works and employment programs, or in the 1940s, when the Second World War forced them to promote public ownership and production—their actions can often illuminate possibilities and even policies that can be adopted by governments with radically different aims (which is not to say that state policies are ever class-neutral).

The situation in Europe following the end of the Second World War offers another example. European governments at the time were under great pressure from the United States to liberalize their economies. Their response, specifically the creation of the European Payments Union, offers important and positive lessons for those supportive of the ALBA initiative.

Background to the Formation of the EPU

For complex historical reasons, the developed capitalist countries of Europe faced economic challenges in the immediate postwar period that were remarkably similar to those faced by many third world countries today. U.S. government and business elites wanted to establish an international economic system underpinned by freely traded (convertible) currencies and liberalized trade. This posed a problem for European governments.

European economies had been greatly weakened by the war. As a consequence, their import needs were far greater than their export capacities. If European governments accepted U.S. demands for liberalization, their countries would quickly run large trade deficits. Since they lacked sufficient foreign exchange, they would be forced to implement austerity measures (to reduce the demand for imports), leading to a downward spiral of production and employment.

Such an outcome would be nothing new for most third world countries, whose governments have routinely been pressured into liberalizing international economic activity. However, despite its weakened position, Europe was not the third world. In particular, European governments retained considerable negotiating leverage with U.S. policymakers.

Europe's importance as part of the capitalist core meant that U.S. elites could not be indifferent to the political ramifications of Europe's economic choices. European workers could be expected to strongly oppose the austerity required to restore trade balances if European governments embraced liberalization. Both U.S. and European elites feared that this opposition could dramatically strengthen the already considerable influence of the left throughout the region.

Equally important, European governments managed economies that were already heavily regulated, which meant that they had tools in place to control trade directly if they decided to resist U.S. pressure. Controls were first introduced during the Great

Depression; among the most effective were quantitative restrictions on imports. For example, as of 1937, almost all German and Italian imports, more than half of those of France, Switzerland, and Austria, and approximately one-quarter of those of Belgium and the Netherlands, were subject to quota restrictions.[6] The outbreak of the Second World War led to a further tightening of restrictions on trade. Many currencies ceased to be convertible for both residents and non-residents.

Under these conditions, European governments found that the easiest way to organize trade was through bilateral agreements. By the end of 1947, more than two hundred such agreements were in effect, accounting for more than 60 percent of Western European trade.[7]

European elites did not oppose a return to a fully multilateralized capitalist world system; after all, they had greatly benefited from its past operation. Their concern was that under existing conditions they were not well placed to benefit from its revival. At the same time, they were also aware that the status quo was far from satisfactory. The controls that enabled European governments to regulate economic activity made it harder to restore business confidence (and, by extension, growth) and strengthened the left's demands for a broader structural transformation of existing capitalist institutions and relations.

In short, European elites desperately needed an alternative strategy, one that would support regional economic revitalization by providing protection from U.S. competition while simultaneously weakening obstacles to Europe's eventual participation in a renewed multilateral system. The U.S. government, for its own reasons, eventually agreed to support the search for such a strategy.

The EPU

OEEC governments negotiated several agreements in the late 1940s, supported by Marshall Plan aid, that were designed to promote intra-European currency convertibility and trade liberalization. But their limited scope yielded meager gains.[8] Frustrated by the slow pace of change, the U.S. government eventually took charge. In October 1949, after the State Department overcame Treasury Department objections, Marshall Plan director Paul Huffman called on the OEEC Council to take concrete steps toward the creation of a single integrated European market. Two months later, one of his assistants put forward a plan for achieving this outcome. Significantly, this plan served as the basis for the EPU agreement that was approved by OEEC members on July 7, 1950.[9]

The EPU broke with bilateralism by establishing a highly regulated multilateral payments system. Trade continued to be controlled as before, but now, if intra-OEEC and approved by the relevant governments, it could proceed without regard to national holdings of foreign exchange. Previously, for example, if a Dutch importer was granted permission by the Dutch government to import tractors and decided to purchase German ones, the trade could be completed only if the Dutch central bank held sufficient German marks. Often that was not the case, which meant that the importer had no choice but to import tractors from another country, one whose currency was held in ample supply by the Dutch central bank.

The EPU changed this. Under the new system, the Dutch importer would simply pay its central bank in Dutch guilders, the Dutch central bank would inform the German central bank of the importer's desired purchase, and (assuming the German government approved the sale) the German central bank would pay its exporter in marks. The German central bank would record a surplus position in Dutch guilders in its account with the Dutch central bank, and the Dutch central bank would record a deficit in German marks in its account with the German central bank.

At the end of every month, each central bank would calculate its net position with every other central bank—using existing national exchange rates—and convert the balance into its own currency. Then it would total its separate national balances and report an overall final balance in its own currency to the Bank of International Settlements (BIS), which operated as the EPU's financial agent. The BIS would take these national balances, convert them into EPU units of account, or "ecus," and calculate final balances.[10] In this way, EPU member nations registered monthly deficits or surpluses with the EPU itself, not other member nations. Because the EPU was a closed system, the sum of all intra-EPU trade balances had to equal zero.

Finally, the BIS would determine the payment required to settle these outstanding monthly balances. The amount depended on the value of each country's cumulative debt or surplus (since the start of the EPU), relative to its assigned quota. And its assigned quota was set equal to 15 percent of its total visible and invisible trade with other member nations and their monetary areas in 1949.

A debtor country with a monthly deficit would have that deficit fully covered by EPU credit as long as its cumulative debt remained equal to or less than 20 percent of its assigned quota. As monthly trade results pushed a country's cumulative debt above the 20 percent mark, a growing percentage of its monthly balance had to be paid in gold (or U.S. dollars). If a country's cumulative debt exceeded its quota, it was obligated to pay its entire monthly deficit in gold (see Table 6.1).

Surplus countries were treated somewhat differently. A surplus country with a monthly surplus would have to give its full surplus in credit to the EPU if its total surplus was less than 20 percent of its assigned quota. However, rather than receive a growing percentage of its monthly surpluses in gold as its total surplus grew beyond the 20 percent mark, its gold share was set at a constant 50 percent (see Table 6.1). It was left up to the Managing Board to determine how the monthly surplus of a country with a cumulative surplus larger than its quota would be compensated.

Of course, national trade balances fluctuated. Countries with cumulative surpluses sometimes ran monthly deficits, and countries with cumulative deficits sometimes posted monthly surpluses. In such cases the "last-in, first-out" principle applied: the

TABLE 6.1: EPU Settlement Terms

For Cumulative Debts or Surpluses	Deficits are Covered		Surpluses are Covered	
	by Gold	by Credit	by Gold	by Credit
0% to 20% of quota	0%	100%	0%	100%
20% to 40% of quota	20%	80%	50%	50%
40% to 60% of quota	40%	60%	50%	50%
60% to 80% of quota	60%	40%	50%	50%
80% to 100% of quota	80%	20%	50%	50%
Cumulative total	40%	60%	40%	60%

Source: Robert Triffin, *Monetary Reconstruction in Europe* (New York: Carnegie Endowment for International Peace, 1952), 285.

most recent credits to or from the EPU were erased and the most recent gold paid to or received from the EPU was returned.

Depending on how the deficits and surpluses were allocated across countries, EPU gold receipts from deficit countries could be, and sometimes were, less than required gold payments to surplus countries. Therefore, the EPU needed a capital fund, and this was provided by the United States at the time of the EPU's launch.

It is easy to imagine why deficit countries embraced this system—it provided them with credit and reduced their potential dependence on any one creditor country. But there were also benefits for surplus countries. For example, the system assured them that they would receive gold payments for their exports, regardless of the foreign exchange holdings of the importing country. The EPU clearing mechanism also promoted trade as well as trade liberalization (discussed below), both of which disproportionately benefited surplus countries.

The EPU Managing Board

Key to the operation of the EPU was the Managing Board, and there were serious disagreements between U.S. and OEEC negotiators over its proposed authority. The U.S. government wanted a "supranational" Managing Board with the power to discipline governments whose policies were viewed as a threat to the region's achievement of currency convertibility and trade liberalization. The OEEC countries did not agree, and they prevailed. The Managing Board was limited to making policy recommendations (which could be carried by majority vote) to the OEEC Council, where the board had to receive unanimous support from all the member governments before they could take effect.

Struggles also took place over the composition of the Managing Board. The IMF strongly disapproved of the EPU project, fearing that it would strengthen regionalism, which was contrary to the IMF mission of promoting universal liberalization. In particular, the IMF feared that the Managing Board would become a powerful rival. At a minimum, the IMF wanted a voting seat on the Managing Board. OEEC countries disagreed, and won this battle as well. In 1953 the OEEC Council did agree to allow an IMF representative to attend Managing Board meetings, but only as an observer.

These victories by OEEC governments stand as tribute to the fact that European elites continued to enjoy considerable unity and collective capacity to defend their interests. At the same time, it is important to acknowledge that European and U.S. elites shared a common commitment to rebuilding a strong, functioning global capitalist order. No doubt this made it easier for the United States to yield to European wishes.

It was originally assumed that because the EPU clearing system would automatically ensure regional stability and growth, the work of the Managing Board would be routine. However, this assumption was quickly challenged by events; the enormous differences in national economic circumstances almost immediately produced significant trade imbalances that could not be handled by normal EPU operations. As a consequence, the Managing Board, with the support of the OEEC Council, was forced to take the lead in developing responses to a series of crises.

Challenges and Responses

The Achilles' heel of the EPU was its asymmetrical treatment of surplus and deficit countries. Surplus countries enjoyed a structural advantage over deficit countries, and there was nothing in the EPU clearing mechanism that forced surplus countries to adjust their policies. As a result, deficit countries bore the full weight of adjustment, even if their deficit was exacerbated by the policies of surplus countries.

This was an especially serious problem for the EPU system because, given its regional structure, total intra-regional surpluses had to be balanced by equivalent intra-regional deficits. Thus if one or more member countries succeeded in recording large, continuous trade surpluses, it was likely that one or more member countries would be recording large, continuous trade deficits. If these debtor nations suffered too great a loss of reserves, they might well be forced into restoring restrictions on regional transactions, thereby threatening the EPU project.

John Maynard Keynes worried about this very same problem in the early 1940s while working on a draft proposal for a world bank. He sought to overcome it by recommending the following: all countries were to have accounts at the world bank, which would record their deficits and surpluses with all other members. The bank would have the authority to create its own international reserve currency, the bancor; it would extend credit in the form of bancors to debtor countries up to an established quota limit. All countries with large trade imbalances relative to their assigned quotas (regardless of whether surplus or deficit) would be required to pay interest penalties to the bank. Because penalties increased as the imbalances grew larger, both deficit and surplus countries would have a material interest in adjusting their respective policies to achieve more balanced trade.[11]

The OEEC created an EPU that differed from Keynes's draft proposal for a world bank in two important ways. First, the OEEC chose not to create a new international reserve currency;

the ecu functioned only as a virtual unit of account. Second, the OEEC did not create any mechanism to force surplus countries to adjust their policies in the interest of achieving balanced trade patterns.[12] Indeed, quite the opposite was true. Deficit countries were required to pay interest on the credit advanced to them by the EPU, and surplus countries were paid interest on the credit they advanced to the EPU.

Not surprisingly, then, the first crisis to confront the EPU Managing Board was the result of a large and growing trade deficit. The German government had unsuccessfully tried to control its deficit. It had sharply raised interest rates in an attempt to slow down economic activity and, by extension, imports. It had also tried more direct measures to reduce its trade deficit. For example, it required businesses seeking an import license to make a bank deposit equal to 50 percent of the cost of the goods to be imported. Import licenses were required, even if the goods were not subject to quotas.

Despite these efforts, by October 1950, Germany's cumulative debt had grown so large that it was close to exhausting its quota. If this happened, the government would have to pay dollars to finance the country's future monthly deficits, something that it could not do for very long because of a foreign exchange shortage. The EPU Managing Board recognized that it would have to act quickly or Germany would be forced to take even more drastic actions. And, if Germany dramatically tightened its trade regime, other countries would find their own exports affected, which would make it harder for them to keep their markets open. The likely result would be a regression to the previous system of bilateral trade arrangements.

In December 1950, determined to avoid this outcome, the Managing Board granted Germany a special credit. The Managing Board also called on the other member countries to do what they could to increase their imports of German goods.

By February 1951, Germany had used most of its special credit. The German government, with the support of the Managing Board, suspended its trade liberalization efforts and stopped issuing import licenses. Even more striking, the OEEC Council, responding to a Managing Board recommendation, decided on the following:

> If Germany's payments position improved enough to warrant issuance of new import licenses these were to be allocated according to principles interpreted by a Mediation Group of three independent experts appointed by the Council. Taking account of "the essential needs of the German economy," the Mediation Group was to recommend allocation of licenses "primarily in favor of Denmark, Greece, Iceland, the Netherlands, Norway and Turkey," countries which were heavily in debt to the EPU and which would suffer particularly from a cut in German imports.[13]

Germany's situation did improve enough for the Managing Board to recommend resumption of import licensing, but only according to the terms noted above. The OEEC Council, following Mediation Group recommendations, set an upper limit for the total monthly value of German imports. Within that total, upper limits were established for the value of imports for different categories of goods; the biggest division was between the imports of goods that had previously been liberalized and those that remained restricted by quota.

The countries singled out by the Mediation Group, which were themselves struggling to finance their deficits, were given preferential rights to supply Germany with goods that had previously been liberalized. Imports of goods that remained regulated were to be divided among all suppliers according to another Council-determined formula based on past trade patterns. Germany was given the right to make minor adjustments to the plan and could appeal to the OEEC Council if major ones were necessary.

Germany was not the only country to suffer large deficits. Before the end of EPU's first year, Austria, Greece, and Iceland had also exhausted their quotas and been given additional credits. The

Netherlands faced a similar problem, but rather than aid, it was granted a larger quota.

What is perhaps most significant about the actions described above is that they demonstrate that the Managing Board and OEEC Council were willing and able to act in defense of the collective interest as defined by the objectives of the EPU. Said differently, member governments demonstrated an impressive willingness to yield significant power to higher-level bodies, power that enabled these bodies to shape national trade activity. Equally noteworthy, this power was used—most aggressively in the case of Germany— to impose a system of regulation that (temporarily) reversed past liberalization efforts.

New challenges arose in the second year. In response to growing trade deficits, France, in February 1952, suspended its trade liberalization and tightened its foreign exchange controls. However, the most serious threats to the system in this period came from surplus countries, in particular Belgium. At the end of July 1951, Belgium's cumulative surplus almost equaled its quota. And, as noted previously, the EPU had no established rules specifying how countries in such a position should be compensated for their monthly trade surpluses.

Rather than compensate Belgium in gold for its surpluses and risk exhausting the EPU's hard currency holdings, the Managing Board decided temporarily to increase Belgium's quota. This meant that future Belgium surpluses would continue to be settled on the basis of 50 percent gold and 50 percent credit. Belgium continued to register strong surpluses into 1952, and the Managing Board successfully pressured it into five additional quota expansions.

Rather than allow this situation to continue, the OEEC Council pressed the Belgian government to change its economic policies. Eventually, the Belgian government yielded; it limited the nation's exports to other member countries and restricted imports from outside Europe to encourage greater regional purchases.

Although the agreement creating the EPU gave the organization only a two-year life, it was renewed annually seven additional times. These renewals were far from automatic, however. The negotiations were marked by growing tensions, especially between surplus and deficit countries, with the former increasingly unhappy about being forced to accept credits rather than hard currency for their surpluses.

European governments had always viewed the EPU as a necessary but transitional arrangement. Perhaps not surprisingly, the United Kingdom, because of its interest in restoring the pound as an international currency, and the major creditor countries—Belgium, Switzerland, the Netherlands, and Germany, which had overcome its previous trade problems—were the most eager to terminate the EPU. In 1955 these countries succeeded in winning OEEC Council approval of the European Monetary Agreement (EMA), which called for termination of the EPU when countries holding more than half the total EPU quota requested it. The EMA did not establish a successor regime, only a financial safety net, the European Fund, to assist countries that found currency convertibility difficult to finance.

Finally, on December 27, 1958, Belgium, France, Germany, Italy, Luxembourg, the Netherlands, and the United Kingdom informed the OEEC Council that they were ready to end the EPU. The next day, all member countries (except Greece, Iceland, and Turkey) restored external convertibility for non-resident holders of their currencies, which meant that those living outside the EPU area could now freely exchange any European currency they acquired through current account activity for any other European currency or dollars. The Council officially approved implementation of the EMA on December 30, 1958; the final business of the EPU was concluded on January 15, 1959.

Achievements of the EPU

The EPU multilateral clearing system proved remarkably successful in promoting intra-regional trade and national growth. In particular, it encouraged trade by greatly reducing Europe's need for scarce foreign exchange. As Table 6.2 illustrates, over the system's roughly eight years of operation, 70 percent of all bilateral trade imbalances were settled by automatic EPU adjustments, as measured by the sum of balances cleared by multilateral offsetting compensation and compensation through time.

More generally, by structuring balance of payments accounts around the EPU rather than individual nations, and providing a number of mechanisms for harmonizing trade between surplus and deficit countries, the system also helped reduce austerity pressures on deficit countries, with beneficial consequences for the surplus countries as well. The economic gains achieved over this period are indeed striking:

> In the OEEC area as a whole, gross national product grew, in real terms, by 48 percent and industrial output by 65 percent during the EPU period. This corresponded to annual compound rates of growth of about 5 and 7 percent respectively. No precedent exists in the records of market economies for such intense growth in so many countries over so long a period of years. The United States did not quite reach that rate even in the years from 1940 to 1949, when it mobilized a depressed economy for war and postwar reconstruction.[14]

For European elites, perhaps the most meaningful measure of the EPU's success was the region's return to a position of relative dominance in a renewed liberalized international economic order. European countries began the postwar period forced to regulate international economic activity largely because of a shortage of dollars. The EPU supported European recovery in part by shielding European producers from U.S. imports. European exports to the dollar area were not, however, similarly restricted.

As Europe recovered, so did its dollar exports and dollar reserves. Europe's reserves, which totaled $10.5 billion at the end of 1945 and $10.1 billion at the end of 1951, were $17.7 billion by the end

TABLE 6.2: EPU Settlement of Bilateral Trade Deficits and Surpluses

Year	Multilateral Offsetting Compensation	Compensation through Time	Dollars/Gold	Credit
1950–51	47%	16%	7%	19%
1951–52	40%	34%	16%	10%
1952–53	54%	37%	7%	2%
1953–54	49%	22%	33%	-4%
1954–55	47%	39%	17%	-3%
1955–56	37%	28%	39%	-3%
1956–57	35%	16%	41%	8%
1957–58	39%	32%	27%	2%
7/1958–12/1958	40%	12%	38%	12%
7/1950–12/1958	43%	27%	23%	6%

Source: OEEC, *Final Report of the EPU Managing Board, Final Period 1st July–27th December 1958* (Paris: OEEC, 1959), 47.

of 1957.[15] By the end of the decade, Western European economies had become strong enough to earn all the dollars they needed. In fact, Europeans began dumping dollars for gold, a clear indicator that dollars were no longer scarce. Significantly, 1958 marked the first year in which the United States suffered a major decline in its gold stock, raising international concerns about whether the U.S. government would be able to defend the existing dollar-gold exchange rate. The United States would soon be forced to seek European assistance to defend the existing international system.

The EPU and Trade Liberalization

The establishment of the EPU reflected the priority OEEC governments gave to achieving intra-European currency convertibility. Although important in its own right, OEEC governments also saw the EPU as a critical precondition to the achievement of another goal, trade liberalization. In other words, OEEC governments sought the creation of a regionally protected, integrated monetary and trade zone. Thus, shortly after approving the formation of the EPU, they signed another agreement that committed them to reducing their quantitative restrictions on intra-OEEC trade.

In 1952 a Steering Board for Trade, comparable to the EPU Managing Board, was established to oversee the implementation of trade initiatives and promote further liberalization (which referred only to reducing quantitative restrictions on trade, not tariff reductions).[16] European trade liberalization proceeded slowly but steadily over the decade. By the end of 1956, 89 percent of private intra-European trade had been liberalized. The combined effect of the EPU settlement system and intra-regional quota liberalization "contributed to a spectacular increase in intra-European trade. With 1949 equal to 100, the volume of intra-European imports rose to 141 in 1950, to 151 in 1951, and, by 1956, had climbed to 226."[17]

For years, liberalization was strictly a European affair. For example, "At the beginning of 1953, only 11 percent of Western European (OEEC) imports from the United States and Canada were free from quantitative restrictions. By the beginning of 1954, this figure had been raised to 32 percent, by April 1, 1955, to 47 percent, and by June 30, 1956, to 59 percent. In 1957, almost two-thirds of Western European imports from the United States and Canada were free from quantitative restrictions."[18]

Though OEEC governments had made great strides toward their goal of trade liberalization, it is important to recognize that at the close of 1958, some thirteen years after the end of the Second World War, approximately 10 percent of intra-European trade and 30 percent of European trade with the United States and Canada remained restricted by quota. Moreover, tariff levels stayed high. It was not until 1961 that the leading OEEC countries fully liberalized their trade with the dollar area.

Development Lessons

The EPU experience offers many valuable lessons for third world countries pursuing development, especially those in ALBA that seek to create their own regionally protected, integrated currency and trade zones. One lesson is that states can effectively impose strong regulations over international economic activity for an extended period of time. Mainstream economists strongly criticize third world countries for trying to implement tough quantitative controls when faced with serious balance of payments problems. Yet, as we have seen, European governments resisted opening their economies to market competition, choosing instead to rely on an ever-expanding system of state controls.

Another lesson is that it is possible to construct a cooperative development process that does promote the collective interests of its participants. As highlighted above, European governments did join together to create mechanisms that promoted regional integration and economic rebuilding, most importantly the EPU. During periods of crisis, EPU governing institutions proved willing and able to make decisions in the broader interest of the community, even when that meant implementing policies that discriminated against the stronger economies.

Finally, the EPU experience strongly suggests that it may be a mistake to conceive of development solely as a national project. European countries, among the most powerful countries in the world, faced enormous rebuilding challenges at the close of the Second World War. Rather than go it alone, they coalesced around a plan for a long-term, protected cooperative development process that was anchored by the EPU.

Significantly, many third world countries are already enmeshed in a form of economic integration, some by choice and others by compulsion. It is a neoliberal integration designed to promote greater liberalization, deregulation, privatization, and capital mobility. As a consequence, its achievements are best measured by exports, inflows of foreign direct investment, and corporat profitability, not social gains. In some cases, this process of integration has been formalized: examples include NAFTA, AFTA, and Mercosur.[19]

The postwar European approach to integration, although still shaped by capitalist imperatives, was very different—more protected and cooperative, and thus development oriented. No doubt its embrace by European governments is best explained by historically specific conditions. Regardless, the operation of the EPU offers a productive starting point for thinking about the structures and mechanisms required to anchor an alternative, progressive integration project.

The EPU experience, however, does not offer a precise blueprint for today's third world countries. For example, whereas European governments sought to structure a slow, sustained regional liberalization process, third world governments will need to structure a regionalization process that enhances their respective planning and regulatory capacities. And, whereas the OEEC Council rejected any overall regional planning, along with any mechanism to promote regional balance by forcing adjustment of surplus as well as deficit country trade patterns, these decisions are the opposite of what a successful third world effort would require.

At present, ALBA offers the most promising, if not the only meaningful attempt at cooperative development anywhere in the world. Consistent with the organization's state-centered orientation, most ALBA activities have, to this point, involved bilaterally negotiated agreements between state enterprises in which one country provides the other with goods, technical or financial support for investments in core industries, affordable energy resources, or assistance in delivering critical social services. However, ALBA's declaration of intent to create an integrated trade and currency zone, backed by a new regional currency, appears to signal a serious commitment by member countries to move beyond existing bilateral efforts to foster a regional development process.

Significantly, ALBA's early steps to concretize its People's Trade Agreement contain echoes of the EPU experience. Although negotiations on zone operating principles continue, ALBA appears close to establishing a Sucre system with a regional monetary council, a central clearing house, a regional reserve and emergency fund, and the Sucre itself.

Several countries have already deposited agreed-upon amounts of their respective national currencies into a special Sucre fund. These monies are then converted into Sucre. At this point, the Sucre exists only as a virtual unit of account, with an exchange value of $1.25, and is being used only for targeted trade of specific commodities. The first Sucre-denominated transaction, involving Venezuelan rice exports to Cuba, occurred in January 2010. Bolivia, Nicaragua, and Ecuador also have plans to engage in Sucre-denominated trade.[20] ALBA's long-term goal is for the Sucre to become an international reserve currency much like the euro.

Drawing further on the EPU experience, one could imagine the ALBA cooperative development process unfolding as follows: the ALBA Council would first select several key development drivers—perhaps health care, education, energy, and food production—to serve as focal points for protected regional activity. Then it would encourage the adoption of many of the same currency and trade policies employed by EPU countries to further the creation of regionally anchored health, education, energy, and food production systems. If structured properly, these systems would provide benefits to every member country—for example, offering access to affordable medicine and sustainably produced agricultural goods—and ensure that every member country had a role to play in its operation through an assigned area of specialization.

Although in an ideal world each driver would be anchored by a different country, in reality most ALBA members do not yet have the research-production-service core capacities necessary to play such a role. However, Cuba is well placed to advance regional efforts in health care and basic education, and Venezuela is capable of doing the same with energy. ALBA countries, as a group, have the ability to make meaningful strides toward the achievement of regional food sovereignty.

The aim of such an effort would not be the creation of identical systems in each country—which would be impossible even if desired—but rather a collective effort to ensure that critical goods and services are sustainably produced and shared within the ALBA community. For example, in the case of health care, structured trade could promote the development and regional distribution of Cuban pharmaceuticals. At the same time, other member countries could support the strengthening of the Cuban health system by providing Cuba with difficult to obtain inputs, such as lab equipment, specialty vehicles, and computer systems and services. Similarly, ALBA governments could increase their capital contributions to the ALBA bank and direct it to fund the sustainable production of basic food items in member countries, transportation networks to distribute them, and state-owned marketing outlets in each country to sell them at affordable prices.[21]

Though successful national development ultimately depends on choices made by the citizens of the nation itself, collective projects like the EPU or ALBA have a critical role to play. Complex struggles are under way in Bolivia, Cuba, and Venezuela to define and shape a socialist political economy appropriate for the twenty-first century.[22] Significantly, the operation and evolution of ALBA could prove pivotal in tipping the balance of forces toward a favorable outcome. ALBA initiatives, such as the People's Trade Agreement, have the potential to offer these countries an important degree of economic assistance and political protection, both of which are absolutely necessary to help counter U.S. opposition. Advances in these countries would, in turn, likely have a powerful and positive effect on the direction of the ALBA project itself, as well as development choices in the other member countries.

Economic development is a multifaceted and difficult process. Yet there is much we can learn from both the EPU experience and the ALBA project—and good reasons to be optimistic about the future.

Notes

1. The Internationalization of Production and Its Consequences

1. United Nations Conference on Trade and Development, *World Investment Report 2011: Non-Equity Modes of International Production and Development* (New York: United Nations, 2011), 24.
2. Ibid.
3. For an extended discussion of how capitalism's laws of motion drive the concentration and centralization and, by extension, the internationalization of production through the growth of transnational corporations, see John Bellamy Foster, Robert W. McChesney, and R. Jamil Jonna, "Internationalization of Monopoly Capital," *Monthly Review* 63/2 (June 2011).
4. Richard Westra, "South Korea Déjà Vu," *Journal of Contemporary Asia* 40/2 (May 2010): 330.
5. United Nations Conference on Trade and Development, *World Investment Report 1991: The Triad in Foreign Direct Investment* (New York: United Nations, 1991), iii.
6. Ibid., 4.
7. Paul Burkett and Martin Hart-Landsberg, *Development, Crisis, and Class Struggle: Learning from Japan and East Asia* (New York: St. Martin's Press, 2000), chaps. 9 and 12.
8. United Nations Conference on Trade and Development, *World Investment Report 1999: Foreign Direct Investment and the Challenge of Development* (New York: United Nations, 1999), 9.
9. Ibid.
10. Asian Development Bank, *Asian Development Outlook 2011: South-South Economic Links* (Philippines: Asian Development Bank, 2011), 49.
11. United Nations Conference on Trade and Development, *World Investment Report 2011*, 3.

12. Ibid., xx–xxi.
13. Ibid., 134.
14. Ibid., xx–xxi.
15. Ibid., 134.
16. Ibid., 159.
17. Ibid., 134–36.
18. Yuqing Xing and Neal Detert, "How the iPhone Widens the United States Trade Deficit with the People's Republic of China," Asian Development Bank Institute, Working Paper Series 257 (December 2010), 2.
19. Ibid., 5.
20. Kenneth L. Kraemer, Greg Linden, and Jason Dedrick, "Capturing Value in Global Networks: Apple's iPad and iPhone," Working Papers, University of California Irvine (July 2011), 4.
21. The distortions created by maintaining a nation-state focus in the face of the internationalization of production are also highlighted by the framing of environmental tensions between developed and developing countries, the United States and China in particular. One argument made by the United States and other developed countries against a renewal of the Kyoto Agreement is that the Protocol does not include binding emission reduction targets on countries like China that are major producers of greenhouse gases. However, if we consider emissions generated in a given territory as a result of both production and consumption rather than simply of production, we get a very different picture of responsibilities. Since a growing share of Asian manufacturing production is exported to developed countries, the calculation of territorial emissions based simply on production greatly overstates Asian responsibility and understates developed country responsibility. Thus emission reduction cannot fairly or productively be approached solely through the use of national/territorial mandates. We need to recognize that progress in achieving environmentally sustainable economic relations will require national changes that also confront and transform contemporary capitalist globalization dynamics. See Glen P. Petersa, Jan C. Minx, Christopher L. Weberd, and Ottmar Edenhoferc, "Growth in Emission Transfers via International Trade from 1990 to 2008," Proceedings of the National Academy of Sciences 108/21 (2011).
22. Kraemer, Linden, and Dedrick, "Capturing Value in Global Networks," 6.
23. Daniel Gross, "Invest Globally, Stagnate Locally," *New York Times,* April 2, 2006.
24. Ibid.
25. Ibid.
26. Ibid.
27. Joe Weisenthal, "Chart of the Day: What Percent of Corporate Profits Come from Overseas?," *Businessinsider.com,* May 17, 2011.
28. Peter Coy and Jesse Drucker, "Profits on an Overseas Holiday," *Bloomberg Businessweek*, March 21, 2011, 66.
29. Foster, McChesney, and Jonna, "Internationalization of Monopoly Capital."

30.   As Paul Sweezy noted, the growth in transnational production, stagnation of core economies, and the financialization of the accumulation process are all "intricately related." See Paul M. Sweezy, "More (or Less) on Globalization," *Monthly Review* 49/4 (September 1997).

31.   United Nations Conference on Trade and Development, *World Investment Report 1991*, 28.

32.   Ibid, 24.

33.   Gerard Greenfield, "The WTO Agreement on Trade-Related Investment Measures (TRIMS)," *Canadian Center for Policy Alternatives* 2/1, Briefing Paper Series: Trade and Investment (January 2001).

34.   For more on the WTO and its many agreements see *Public Citizen*'s Global Trade Watch, http://www.citizen.org/trade/.

35.   Chapter 3 in this book presents a critical examination of the class forces promoting the Korea-U.S. Free Trade Agreement, governmental efforts to secure its passage, and the efforts of both South Korean and U.S. labor and social movements to defeat it.

36.   Mi Park, "Framing Free Trade Agreements: The Politics of Nationalism in the Anti Neoliberal Globalization Movement in South Korea," *Globalizations* 6/4 (2009): 455.

37.   United Nations Conference on Trade and Development, *World Investment Report 2011*, 100.

38.   The share of state actions encouraging foreign direct investment declined over the 2000s. For example, in 2000, 70 countries introduced 150 changes with 147, or 98 percent, of them liberalizing or promoting foreign investment. The decline is largely due to the growth in restrictions placed on foreign direct investments in both agribusiness and extractive industries by several Latin American governments. See ibid., 94.

39.   Ibid., xvii.

40.   Asian Development Bank, *Asian Development Outlook 2010: The Future of Growth in Asia* (Philippines: Asian Development Bank, 2010), 38.

41.   Ibid.

42.   Asian Development Bank, *Asian Development Outlook 2009: Rebalancing Asia's Growth* (Philippines: Asian Development Bank, 2009), 96.

43.   Ibid.

44.   Ibid., 97.

45.   Prema-chandra Athukorala and Arhanun Kohpaiboon, "Intra-Regional Trade in East Asia: The Decoupling Fallacy, Crisis and Policy Challenges," Arndt-Corden Division of Economics, Australian National University College of Asia and the Pacific, Working Paper No. 2009/09 (August 2009), 6.

46.   Prema-chandra Athukorala, "Asian Trade Flows: Trends, Patterns, and Projections," Asian Development Bank, Economics Working Paper No. 241 (January 2011), 17.

47.   Prema-chandra Athukorala, "Production Networks and Trade Patterns: East Asia in a Global Context," Arndt-Corden Division of Economics, Australian National University College of Asia and the Pacific, Working

Paper No. 2009/15 (October 2009), 13.

48. Asian Development Bank, *Asian Development Outlook 2008: Workers in Asia* (Philippines: Asian Development Bank, 2008), 22.

49. Athukorala and Kohpaiboon, "Intra-Regional Trade in East Asia," 33.

50. Asian Development Bank, *Asian Development Outlook 2009*, 97.

51. Prema-chandra Athukorala, "The Rise of China and East Asian Export Performance: Is the Crowding-Out Fear Warranted?," Arndt-Corden Division of Economics, Australian National University College of Asia and the Pacific, Working Paper No. 2007/10 (September 2007), 18–19.

52. Asian Development Bank, *Asian Development Outlook 2007: Growth Amid Change* (Philippines: Asian Development Bank, 2007), 69.

53. Ibid., 70.

54. United Nations Conference on Trade and Development, *Trade and Development Report 2010* (New York: United Nations, 2010), 39.

55. Prema-chandra Athukorala and Nobuaki Yamashita, "Global Production Sharing and Sino-U.S. Trade Relations," *China and World Economy* 17/3 (2009): 41.

56. Ibid., 44–45.

57. Ibid., 42.

58. This gain comes at a steep price. East Asia's skyrocketing exports of manufactures has choked off Latin American and Sub-Saharan African efforts at industrial development, renewing their past dependence on primary commodity exports. See Osvaldo Rosales, "Trade Competition from China," *Americas Quarterly* (Winter 2012).

59. "Crowded Out: Chinese Demand Had Ended a Century of Steadily Falling Raw-Material Costs for Rich-World Consumers," *The Economist*, September 24, 2011.

60. Montfort Mlachila and Misa Takebe, "FDI from BRICs to LICs: Emerging Growth Driver?," Working Paper WP/11/178, International Monetary Fund (July 2011).

61. United Nations Conference on Trade and Development, *Trade and Development Report 2010*, 40.

62. Ibid., 43.

63. Ibid.

64. Ibid., 41.

65. John Bellamy Foster and Fred Magdoff, *The Great Financial Crisis: Causes and Consequences* (New York: Monthly Review Press, 2009).

66. United Nations Conference on Trade and Development, *Trade and Development Report 2010*, 44.

67. Ibid., 45.

68. Ibid., 7.

69. Keith Richburg, "In Booming China, How Much Infrastructure Is Too Much?" *Washington Post*, October 22, 2011.

70. Michael Pettis, "My Long-Term Outlook for China and the World," *China Financial Markets* (newsletter), August 17, 2011.

71. For more on the reform process see Martin Hart-Landsberg and Paul Burkett, *China and Socialism: Market Reforms and Class Struggle* (New York: Monthly Review Press, 2005); and "China and Socialism: Engaging the Issues," *Critical Asian Studies* 37/4 (2005).

72. Yılmaz Akyüz, "Export Dependence and Sustainability of Growth in China and the East Asian Production Network," South Center, Research Paper no. 27 (April 2010): 7.

73. Andong Zhu and David M. Kotz, "The Dependence of China's Economic Growth and Investment," *Review of Radical Political Economics* 43/1 (2011): 10.

74. Ibid., 17.

75. John Whalley and Xian Xin, "China's FDI and Non-FDI Economies and the Sustainability of Future High Chinese Growth," National Bureau of Economic Research, Working Paper No. 12249 (May 2006), 9.

76. Ibid., 6.

77. Yuqing Xing, "China's High-Tech Exports: Myth and Reality," National Graduate Institute for Policy Studies, Japan, GRIPS Discussion Paper No. 11-05 (June 2011), 3.

78. Ibid., 8.

79. Tom Miller, "Manufacturing that Doesn't Compute," *Asia Times Online*, November 22, 2006.

80. Xing, "China's High-Tech Exports," 6–7.

81. Dexter Roberts and Pete Engardio, "China's Economy: Behind All the Hype," *Businessweek*, October 22, 2009.

82. For a detailed examination and critical evaluation of China's post-reform transformation see Martin Hart-Landsberg, "China, Capitalist Accumulation, and World Crisis," *Marxism 21* 7/1 (2010); and "The Chinese Reform Experience, A Critical Assessment," *Review of Radical Political Economics* 43/1 (2011).

83. United Nations Conference on Trade and Development, *Trade and Development Report 2002* (New York: United Nations, 2002), 75.

84. Ibid., 76.

85. Erin Lett and Judith Banister, "China's Manufacturing Employment and Compensation Costs: 2002–06," *Monthly Labor Review* 132/4 (April 2009): 32.

86. Ajit K. Ghose, "Employment in China," Employment Analysis Unit, Employment Strategy Papers 2005/14, International Labor Organization (2005), 29.

87. "A Workers' Manifesto for China," *The Economist*, October 11, 2007.

88. Pettis, "My Long-Term Outlook for China and the World."

89. Ibid.

90. *China Labor Bulletin*, "Migrant Workers in China," June 6, 2008.

91. Ibid.; K Kinglun Ngok, "The Changes of Chinese Labor Policy and Labor Legislation in the Context of Market Transition," *International Labor and Working Class History* 73 (2008).

92. Lett and Banister, "China's Manufacturing Employment and Compensation Costs," 34.

93. "New Generation of Migrant Workers Earn an Average of 1,747 Yuan a Month," *Beijing Times*, February 21, 2011.

94. Craig Simons, "New Labor Movement Afoot in China," *Statesmen*, February 4, 2007.

95. "Migrant Workers in China," *China Labor Bulletin*.

96. "Survey of Chinese Workers: Working Conditions in 2010," *China Labor Watch*, March 2011.

97. For more on working and living conditions, especially for workers at foreign-owned electronics factories, see Zhao Hejuan, Lan Fang, Guo Weidi, and Wang Jiapeng, "Dying for a Job: Laboring at a Foxconn Plant," *Caixin online*, June 4, 2010; Robert Weil, "City of Youth, Shenzhen, China," *Monthly Review* 60/2 (June 2008).

98. Charles Duhigg and Keith Bradsher, "How U.S. Lost Out on iPhone Work," *New York Times*, January 21, 2012.

99. Asian Development Bank, *Asian Development Outlook 2009*, 61.

100. See John Bellamy Foster, Robert W. McChesney, and R. Jamil Jonna, "The Global Reserve Army of Labor and the New Imperialism," *Monthly Review* 63/6 (November 2011). As the authors make clear, the profitability of transnational corporate operations depends heavily on the ability of these corporations to shape and exploit a global labor pool.

101. Ibid.

102. Ji-hyun Kim, "Flexibility in Labor Top Priority," *Korea Herald*, May 22, 2004.

103. Yoon-mi Kim, "Korea Suffers First Net FDI Outflow," *Korea Herald*, August 1, 2008.

104. Jung-Myung Oh, "China's Exit Strategies: Effects on Korea and China's Economies," Samsung Economic Research Institute, March 18, 2010, http://www.SERIworld.org.

105. Du-yong Kang, Lee Sang-ho, and Hwang Sunoong, "Korea's Post-Crisis Economic Reliance on China and Policy Suggestions," *Korea Focus*, December 29, 2010.

106. Kyoung-tae Ko, "Poverty Nearly Doubled in the Last Decade," *Korea Herald*, March 19, 2007.

107. Chris Kim, "South Korea: 'Just the First Round' by 'Irregular Workers' at Hyundai Motors," *Links*, December 16, 2010.

108. Dean Baker, "The Housing Bubble and What Greenspan Should Have Done," *Al Jazeera*, January 11, 2012, http://www.aljazeera.com/indepth/opinion/2012/01/2012111122940278108.html.

109. Atif Mian and Amir Sufi, "Housing Bubble Fueled Consumer Spending," Real Time Economics blog, *Wall Street Journal*, June 25, 2009.

110. Louise Story, "Executive Pay," *New York Times*, December 5, 2011.

111. David H. Autor, David Dorn, and Gordon H. Hanson, "The China Syndrome: Local Labor Market Effects of Import Competition in the

United States," MIT Department of Economics, Working Paper, August 2011, 1.

112. Ibid., 21.
113. Ibid., 31.
114. Michael Spence and Sandile Hlatshwayo, "The Evolving Structure of the American Economy and the Employment Challenge," Council on Foreign Relations, Working Paper, March 2011.
115. Ibid., 11–12.
116. Ibid., 12.
117. Ibid., 13.
118. Ibid., 4.
119. Michael Mandel, "A Lost Decade for Jobs," *Businessweek.com*, June 23, 2009.
120. Jed Graham, "10-year Real Wage Growth Worse Than in Depression," *Investors.com*, June 2, 2011, http://news.investors.com/economy/060211-574077-10-year-real-wage-growth-worse-than-in-depression.htm?p=full/.
121. Spence and Hlatshwayo, "The Evolving Structure of the American Economy and the Employment Challenge," 19.
122. Ibid., 23.
123. Stephen S. Roach, "One Number Says It All," *Project-Syndicate.org*, August 25, 2011.
124. John Bellamy Foster and Robert W. McChesney, "Global Stagnation and China," *Monthly Review* 63/9 (February 2012).
125. Joshua Zumbrun, "Margins Widen at U.S. Companies as Wages Lag Behind," *Businessweek.com*, February 28, 2012.
126. Stephen S. Roach, "How Asia Copes with America's Zombie Consumers," *Project-Syndicate.org*, April 27, 2011.
127. Michael Forsythe, "China's Billionaire People's Congress Makes Capitol Hill Look like Pauper," *Bloomberg.com*, February 27, 2012.
128. Asian Development Bank, *Asian Development Outlook 2010 Update: The Future of Growth in Asia* (Philippines: Asian Development Bank, 2010), 51.
129. Hart-Landsberg, "China, Capitalist Accumulation, and World Crisis"; and Foster and McChesney, "Global Stagnation and China."
130. Nouriel Roubini, "China's Bad Growth Bet," *Project-Syndicate.org*, April 14, 2011.
131. For example, it is unclear whether the U.S. economy will undergo further restructuring. Alan Blinder has argued that the United States should expect a new wave of outsourcing. His estimate is that between 30 and 40 million business service jobs are vulnerable. See David Wessel and Bob Davis, "Pain from Free Trade Spurs Second Thoughts," *Wall Street Journal*, March 28, 2007. At the same time, globalization has so weakened the U.S. working class that some U.S. transnational corporations are moving manufacturing jobs back to the United States from Canada to take advantage of lower wages. See James R. Hagerty and Kate Linebaugh, "In U.S., a Cheaper Labor Pool," *Wall Street Journal*, January 6, 2012.

China's situation may also be in flux. Increases in Chinese wages and the appreciation of the Chinese currency have led some transnational corporations to contemplate shifting low-skill manufacturing production to other lower wage countries in Asia.

132. Stephen S. Roach, "Another Asian Wake-Up Call," *Project-Syndicate.org*, November 28, 2011. For more on the causes and consequences of the European crisis see *Research on Money and Finance*, http://www.researchonmoneyandfinance.org/; and Yanis Varoufakis, http://yanisvaroufakis.eu/euro-crisis/.

133. John Chan, "Strike Wave Resumes in China," *World Socialist Web Site*, February 27, 2012, http://www.wsws.org/.

134. "Unity Is Strength: The Workers Movement in China 2009-2011," *China Labor Bulletin*, October 2011.

135. Mobo Gao, *The Battle for China's Past, Mao and the Cultural Revolution* (Ann Arbor, MI: Pluto Press, 2008).

136. Michael D. Yates, ed., *Wisconsin Uprising: Labor Fights Back* (New York: Monthly Review Press, 2012).

2. Neoliberalism: Myths and Reality

This chapter was originally published as Martin Hart-Landsberg, "Neoliberalism: Myths and Reality," Monthly Review 57/11 (April 2006).

1. Quoted in Ha-Joon Chang, *Kicking Away the Ladder: Development Strategy in Historical Perspective* (London: Anthem Press, 2002), 15.

2. William Cline, "Doha Can Achieve Much More than Skeptics Expect," *Finance and Development* (March 2005): 22.

3. For critical analysis of the FTAA, see Martin Hart-Landsberg, "FTAA, The Hydra's New Head," *Against the Current* 15/6 (January–February 2001).

4. For more on the WTO and its many agreements see *Public Citizen*'s Global Trade Watch, http://www.citizen.org/trade/.

5. Significantly, most neoliberal theorists do not include the free movement of people in their argument.

6. Additional discussion of the theoretical weaknesses underlying free-trade theories can be found in Arthur MacEwan, *Neo-Liberalism or Democracy: Economic Strategy, Markets, and Alternatives for the 21st Century* (New York: Zed Press, 1999), chap. 2; Graham Dunkley, *The Free Trade Adventure: The WTO, the Uruguay Round and Globalism—A Critique* (New York: Zed Press, 2000), chap. 6; and Anwar Shaikh, "The Economic Mythology of Neoliberalism," in *Neoliberalism: A Critical Reader*, ed. Alfredo Saad-Filho (London: Pluto Press, 2005).

7. Drusilla Brown, Alan Deardoff, and Robert Stern, *CGE Modeling and Analysis of Multilateral and Regional Negotiating Options*, Discussion Paper 468, University of Michigan School of Public Policy Research Seminar in International Economics (2001), http://www.fordschool.umich.edu/rsie/workingpapers/Papers451-475/r468.pdf.

8. World Bank, *Global Economic Prospects 2002* (Washington, D.C.: World Bank, 2002), xiii.

9. Peter Dorman, *The Free Trade Magic Act*, Briefing Paper (Washington, D.C.: Economic Policy Institute, 2001), 2.

10. World Bank, *Global Economic Prospects 2002*, 166.

11. The restrictions that are eliminated include import tariffs, export subsidies, and domestic production subsidies.

12. World Bank, *Global Economic Prospects 2002*, 167.

13. This result is largely a reflection of the assumptions of the World Bank model. Because the agricultural sector in the third world is protected by relatively high tariffs and assumed inefficient, its liberalization produces the biggest gains for the third world. This view of third world agricultural production ignores all cultural and ecological considerations.

14. Mark Weisbrot and Dean Baker, *The Relative Impact of Trade Liberalization on Developing Countries*, Briefing Paper (Washington, D.C.: Center for Economic and Policy Research, 2002), 1.

15. World Bank, *Global Economic Prospects 2005* (Washington, D.C.: World Bank, 2005), 127.

16. World Bank efforts to model expected global gains in 2015 from a "likely" Doha Round WTO agreement (as opposed to complete trade liberalization) are projected to be just $96 billion, with only $16 billion going to the third world. See Kevin P. Gallagher and Timothy A. Wise, "Back to the Drawing Board: No Basis for Concluding the Doha Round of Negotiations," *RIS Policy Briefs*, April 2008.

17. UNCTAD, *Trade and Development Report 1999* (New York: United Nations, 1999), vi.

18. Ibid.

19. Mark Weisbrot, Dean Baker, and David Rosnick, *The Scorecard on Development: 25 Years of Diminished Progress* (Washington, D.C.: Center for Economic and Policy Research, 2005), 1.

20. UNCTAD, *Trade and Development Report 2002* (New York: United Nations, 2002), 103.

21. Ibid., 63.

22. Ibid., 51.

23. UNCTAD, *Trade and Development Report 2005* (New York: United Nations, 2005), 131.

24. UNCTAD, *Trade and Development Report 2002*, 77.

25. Ibid., 80.

26. For a discussion of the rise of China as a neoliberal success story, see Martin Hart-Landsberg and Paul Burkett, *China and Socialism: Market Reform and Class Struggle* (New York: Monthly Review Press, 2005), esp. chap. 1.

27. Martin Hart-Landsberg and Paul Burkett, "China and the Dynamics of Transnational Accumulation: Causes and Consequences of Global Restructuring," *Historical Materialism* 14/3 (2006), 48–9.

28. "Subsistence Living for Millions of Former State Workers," *China Labor Bulletin*, September 7, 2005.
29. Edward Cody, "Workers In China Shed Passivity, Spate of Walkouts Shakes Factories," *Washington Post*, November 27, 2004.
30. For more discussion on the destructive social consequences of Chinese state policies on working people as well as their growing resistance to these policies, see Hart-Landsberg and Burkett, *China and Socialism*, chap. 3.
31. This restructuring is examined in detail in ibid., chap. 4, and Hart-Landsberg and Burkett, "China and the Dynamics of Transnational Accumulation."

3. Capitalism, the Korea-U.S. Free Trade Agreement, and Resistance
This chapter is an expanded and updated version of Martin Hart-Landsberg, "Capitalism, The Korea-U.S. Free Trade Agreement, and Resistance," Critical Asian Studies 43/3 (2011).

1. The Korea-U.S. Free Trade Agreement was ratified by the U.S. government in October 2011 and the South Korean government in November 2011 and became operational in March 2012. Hereafter, I refer to South Korea as Korea. The U.S. Congress also approved both the Colombia FTA and the Panama FTA in October 2011.
2. Richard Westra, "South Korea Déjà Vu," *Journal of Contemporary Asia* 40 (2010): 330.
3. Prema-Chandra Athukorala and Jayant Menon, *Global Production Sharing, Trade Patterns, and Determinants of Trade Flows in East Asia*, ADB Working Paper Series on Regional Integration, no. 41, Asian Development Bank (January 2010), 3.
4. Hereafter, "components" refers to both parts and components.
5. I rely on the work of Athukorala and Menon, *Global Production Sharing*, who used the UN trade database to estimate the share of components in manufacturing trade for the period 1992 to 2006. Because of shortcomings in the UN categorization system, their estimate of the component trade was limited to an examination of trade data for two categories of products, machinery and transport equipment (SITC 7) and miscellaneous manufacturing (SITC 8). Though these two categories contain the majority of goods currently subject to international production segmentation, the cross-border production of goods in other categories is also growing rapidly, in particular in pharmaceuticals and chemical productions (SITC 5), machine tools and other metal products (SITC 6), and software (SITC 9). Thus, their results should be taken as a minimum estimate of the importance of the trade in components.
6. Ibid., 8–9.
7. Ibid., 10.
8. Asian Development Bank, *Asian Development Outlook 2009* (Manila, Philippines: Asian Development Bank, 2009), 99–100.
9. Asian Development Bank, *Asian Development Outlook 2010 Update* (Manila, Philippines: Asian Development Bank, 2010), 49.

10. Asian Development Bank, *Asian Development Outlook 2009*, 97.

11. Martin Hart-Landsberg, "The U.S. Economy and China: Capitalism, Class and Crisis," *Monthly Review* 61/9 (February 2010): 17.

12. Mi Park, "Framing Free Trade Agreements: The Politics of Nationalism in the Anti-Neoliberal Globalization Movement in South Korea," *Globalization* 6/4 (2009): 452.

13. Ibid.

14. The Korean government is well aware of its dependence. For example, at a January 2011 talk in Washington, D.C., Han Duk-soo, Korean Ambassador to the United States, said: "Passage of the Korea-U.S. FTA will solidify the strategic alliance that has served both our countries so well for the last 60 years. Northeast Asia is a region of dynamic change, both in terms of economics and security. We have seen the reality of that just in the past year: North Korea made two unprovoked and lethal attacks against us. A trade agreement with Korea will send a strong message that the United States intends to stay engaged in the region and retains its influence there." See Third Way.org, "What the U.S.-Korea FTA Means for Americans," January 13, 2011, http://www.thirdway.org/events/36/transcript.

15. Bilaterals.org, "U.S.-Korea," April 2009, http://bilaterals.org/spip.php?rubrique140.

16. The June signing date was critical for U.S. negotiators. Trade Promotion Authority, which gives the U.S. president fast-track negotiating authority over trade agreements, was scheduled to end on the last day of June. Because the KORUS FTA was signed before that deadline, the U.S. Congress did not have the legal right to amend the agreement; it could only vote to approve or disapprove it.

17. For a U.S. government summary of the changes made, see White House, "Increasing U.S. Auto Exports and Growing U.S. Auto Jobs through the U.S.-Korea Trade Agreement," White House Fact Sheet, December 3, 2010, http://www.whitehouse.gov/sites/default/files/fact_sheet_increasing_us_auto_exports_us_korea_free_trade_agreement.pdf. For a Korean view of the revival of the KORUS FTA see Im Pilsoo, "The Revival of the U.S.-Korea FTA, the Global Economic Crisis and U.S. Intentions in East Asia," *People's Solidarity for Social Progress*, September 29, 2010, http://www.pssp.org/eng/?p=93.

18. Jeffrey J. Schott, *Free Trade Agreements and the Future of U.S.-Korean Trade Relations*, KORUS FTA Series, Korea Economic Institute, 2009, 7.

19. For a discussion of these non-tariff barriers and in particular their environmental significance and United States objections to them, see Jung Hyuk-june, "Omitted Auto Tax Revisions Raise Questions About KORUS FTA," *Hankyoreh*, August 25, 2010.

20. For a critical analysis of the agreement's likely effect on U.S. auto employment see Emptywheel, "UAW Sells Out American Workers for 800 Jobs," December 4, 2010, http://emptywheel.firedoglake.com/2010/12/04/uaw-sells-out-american-workers-for-800-jobs/.on.

21. Ron Kirk, "A Trade Agreement that Works for American Businesses and Workers," White House Blog, December 9, 2010, http://www.whitehouse.gov/blog/2010/12/09/a-trade-agreement-works-american-businesses-and-workers.

22. Im Yoon-mi, "Slumping Demand Makes Local Economy More Vulnerable," *Korea Herald*, July 29, 2008; Kwak Young-hoon, "Waning Export Leadership in the Korean Economy," *Korea Focus*, October 2010.

23. Chris Kim, "South Korea: Just the First Round by Irregular Workers at Hyundai Motors," *Links*, December 16, 2010.

24. John Bellamy Foster, "The Financialization of Capital and the Crisis," *Monthly Review* 59/11 (April 2008).

25. U.S. International Trade Commission, *U.S.-Korea Free Trade Agreement: Potential Economy-wide and Selected Sectoral Effects*, Investigation No. TA-2104-24, Publication 3949, corrected printing March 2010, 1.7

26. For a critique of the theory of comparative advantage see Chapter 2 in this book.

27. "Department of Bogus Jobs Statistics," *Eyes on Trade Blog*, August 6, 2010, http://citizen.typepad.com/eyesontrade/2010/08/department-of-bogus-jobs-statistics.html/.

28. Ibid.

29. "U.S. Workers Don't Care if Korea Buys Tomorrow the U.S. Exports Germany Bought Today," *Eyes on Trade Blog*, December 10, 2010, http://citizen.typepad.com/eyesontrade/2010/12/us-workers-dont-care-if-korea-buys-tomorrow-the-us-exports-germany-bought-today.html/.

30. U.S. International Trade Commission, *U.S.-Korea Free Trade Agreement,* F.3.

31. Ibid., xvii.

32. For a more detailed examination of these and other studies see ibid., chap. 7; and Kozo Kiyota and Robert M. Stern, *Economic Effects of a Korea-U.S. Free Trade Agreement*, Special Studies Series, Korea Economic Institute (April 2007).

33. Kiyota and Stern, *Economic Effects of a Korea-U.S. Free Trade Agreement*, 5–6.

34. It is worth emphasizing that despite employing numerous assumptions that impart a strong pro-agreement bias, the projected gains for ratification are surprisingly small.

35. United Nations Conference on Trade and Development, *Trade and Development Report 1999* (New York: United Nations, 1999); Mark Weisbrot, Dean Baker, and David Rosnick, *Scorecard on Development, 25 Years of Diminished Progress,* Center for Economic Policy Research, September 2005.

36. Robert E. Scott, *Trade Policy and Jobs Loss, U.S. Trade Deals with Colombia and Korea Will Be Costly*, EPI Working Paper 289, Economic Policy Institute, 2010.

37. Ibid., 8.

38. Ibid., 9–10.

39. *Public Citizen*, "Lies, Damn Lies and Export Statistics: How Corporate Lobbyists Distort Record of Flawed Trade Deals," September 2010, http:// www.citizen.org/documents/FTA%20Penalty%20Paper%20FINAL1.pdf, 3, 5.

40. U.S. International Trade Commission, *KORUS FTA Final Text*, 2007, http:// www.ustr.gov/trade-agreements/free-trade-agreements/korus-fta/final-text, 17-1.

41. Ibid., 17–4.

42. Labor Advisory Committee for Trade Negotiations and Trade Policy, "Report to the President, the Congress and the United States Trade Representative on the U.S.-Korea (KORUS) Free Trade Agreement," April 27, 2007, http://www.aflcio.org/issues/jobseconomy/globaleconomy/upload/korus_fta07.pdf, 17.

43. Ibid.

44. Lori Wallach, "Obama Administration's Renegotiation of Bush's Korea FTA Must also Fix Investment, Financial Services Terms," *Public Citizen*, June 27, 2010, http://www.citizen.org/documents/Obama's%20Korea%20FTA%20Annoucement-LW%20Statement,%206.27.101.pdf, 1.

45. U.S. International Trade Commission, *KORUS FTA Final Text*, 13.2.

46. Ibid., 13.3.

47. Ibid., 13.12, 13.3.

48. Marwaan Macan-Markar, "Ahead of G-20 Summit, Capital Controls Gain New Currency," Inter Press Service, November 5, 2010, www.ipsnews.net/2010/11/finance-ahead-of-g-20-summit-capital-controls-gain-new-currency/.

49. The "Volcker Rule" was proposed by former United States Federal Reserve chairman Paul Volcker; it was endorsed by President Obama in January 2010. It would prohibit a bank or institution that owns a bank from engaging in proprietary trading of financial instruments for its own direct profit and from owning or investing in a hedge fund or private equity fund.

50. "Korea-U.S. Free Trade Agreement: Problematic Foreign Investor and Financial Deregulation Provisions," *Public Citizen.org*, 2010, http://www.citizen.org/documents/KoreaFTAInvestmentFinancialServices.pdf, 5.

51. U.S. International Trade Commission, *KORUS FTA Final Text*, 13.20.

52. Ibid., 13.5.

53. "Korea-U.S. Free Trade Agreement," *Public Citizen.org*, 4.

54. Ibid. For an examination of the Financial Services chapter that highlights arguments by both defenders and critics, see Mike Alberti, "Could US-Korea Trade Agreement Deter Enhanced Regulation of Financial Services?" *Remapping Debate*, February 2011, http://remappingdebate.org/article/could-us-korea-trade-agreement-deter-enhanced-regulation-financial-services?page=0,3.

55. U.S. International Trade Commission, *KORUS FTA Final Text*, 11.24.

56. Ibid., 11.5.

57. Ibid., 11.2.
58. Ibid., 11.28.
59. Ibid.
60. Ibid.
61. William Glaberson, "NAFTA Invoked to Challenge Court Award," *New York Times*, January 28, 1999.
62. Ibid.
63. "Loewen Loses Controversial NAFTA Case," *Dispute Resolution Journal*, August 1, 2003, www.allbusiness.com/legal/mediation/996963-1.html.
64. For critical perspective on the Pharmaceutical Products and Medical Devices chapter see Sean Flynn and Mike Palmedo, "Initial Response to the KORUS FTA Pharmaceuticals and IP Chapters," Program on Information Justice and Intellectual Property, American University/Washington College of Law, May 25, 2007; Christine Ahn, "The Fight against KORUS FTA, Fight for Humanity, an Interview with Joo-Ho Lee," Korea Policy Institute, February 14, 2011, http://www.kpolicy.org/documents/interviews-opeds/1 10214christineahninterviewjooholee.html.
65. Taking no chances, the U.S. government continues to negotiate trade agreements in secret, at least with regard to the public. Although some 600 transnational corporations are actively and officially helping the U.S. trade representative negotiate the Trans-Pacific Partnership (TPP)—a nine-country free trade agreement involving Australia, Brunei Darussalam, Chile, Malaysia, New Zealand, Peru, Singapore, United States, and Vietnam—the U.S. government refuses to publicly disclose any of the negotiating documents, even to members of the U.S. Congress. In fact, all the governments involved have pledged to keep the negotiating texts secret for at least four years after the agreement goes into force. Leaks suggest the TPP will contain many of the same chapters found in the KORUS FTA. For more on the TPP, see "The Trans-Pacific Free Trade Agreement: NAFTA for the Pacific Rim? " *Public Citizen*, www.citizenstrade.org/ctc/trade-policies/tpp-potential-trade-policy-problems/.
66. Scott, *Trade Policy and Jobs Loss*, 4–5.
67. Ibid., 7.
68. By comparison, the Korean-European Union FTA includes a 55 percent "rules of origin" provision. See John Maggs, "UAW under Fire for Trade Deal Support," *Politico.com*, December 6, 2010, http://www.politico.com/news/stories/1210/46037.html.
69. Significantly, Korean auto workers also opposed this low rules of origin. They feared that it would encourage Korean companies to shift production to China and that U.S. auto producers would boost their market share in Korea using cheap Mexican-produced components. See KCTU, "Why We Oppose the KORUS FTA, "KCTU Position Paper on KORUS FTA," January 2011, http://kctu.org/9928.
70. Steven Greenhouse, "U.S. Union Backing Boosts Korea Trade Pact," *New York Times*, December 8, 2010.
71. Although there is good reason not to take USITC modeling results

seriously, post-December 2010 estimates of the trade consequences of the KORUS FTA by USITC staff economists concluded that the agreement would substantially worsen existing trade deficits in motor vehicles and parts and in other transportation equipment. See "Latest Government Findings Show that the U.S. Trade Deficit May Increase More Under the Korea FTA than Was Previously Thought," *Eyes on Trade Blog*, January 11, 2011, http://citizen.typepad.com/eyesontrade/2011/01/latest-government-findings-show-that-the-us-trade-deficit-may-increase-more-under-the-korea-fta-than.html/.

72. Schott, *Free Trade Agreements and the Future of U.S.-Korean Trade Relations*, 7.

73. Hwang Doo-hyong, "U.S. Business Lobby Supports Obama's Plans for KORUS FTA Ratification," Yonhap News Agency, June 26, 2010.

74. Robert H. Wade, "The Great Slump: What Comes Next?" *Economic and Political Weekly* 44/47 (November 20, 2010): 55.

75. Keith Naughton, "The Happiest Man in Detroit," *Bloomberg Businessweek*, February 7, 2011.

76. The United Food and Commercial Workers is the only other union that has endorsed the KORUS FTA. Apparently it believes that the agreement's promise of greater beef exports will yield significant benefits for its members.

77. "Labor Unions Announce Opposition to Korea Trade Deal," *Eyes on Trade Blog*, December 10, 2010, http://citizen.typepad.com/eyesontrade/2010/12/labor-unions-announce-opposition-to-korea-trade-deal.html/.

78. Richard L. Trumka and Kim Young-Hoon, "Joint Labor Declaration on the U.S.-Korea FTA," September 23, 2010, http://knsi.org/knsi/admin/work/works/Joint+Labor+Declaration+KORUS+FTA+Final.PDF.

79. Ibid.

80. Park, "Framing Free Trade Agreements," 459–60.

81. John W. Miller and Matthew Dalton, "EU Nations Approve Free Trade Pact with South Korea," *Wall Street Journal*, September 17, 2010.

82. "S. Korean biz group urges early approval of Korea-EU FTA," Yonhap News Agency, February 18, 2011.

83. "Free Trade with EU," *Korea Times*, September 19, 2010.

4. After Seattle: Strategic Thinking about Movement Building
This chapter was originally published as Martin Hart-Landsberg, "After Seattle: Strategic Thinking About Movement Building," Monthly Review 52/3 (July-August 2000).

1. See, for example, Doug Henwood, "Reports and Pictures from Seattle," *Left Business Observer*, http://www.panix.com/-dhenwood/Seattle.html; Bill Resnick, "The WTO's Nude World Order," *Against the Current*, March–April 2000; and Jeffrey St. Clair, "Seattle Diary: It's a Gas, Gas, Gas," *New Left Review*, November–December 1999.

2. "WTO's Failure in Bid to Launch Trade Talks Emboldens Protestors," *Wall Street Journal*, December 6, 1999.

3. Unfortunately, many of the same arguments continue to be made. See Martin Hart-Landsberg, "The U.S. Economy and China: Capitalism, Class and Crisis," *Monthly Review* 61/9 (February 2010).

4. Robert E. Scott, "WTO Accession: China Can Wait," *WorkingUSA*, September–October 1999.

5. Ibid., 87.

6. Ibid., 83.

7. Ibid., 84.

8. Ibid.

9. Ibid.

10. See, for example, "China and the WTO—No Hope in Sight," *China Labor Bulletin*, September–October 1999.

11. ILO, "What Are International Labor Standards?" http://www.ilo.org/public/english/standards/norm/whatare/.

12. This remains the situation as of 2013.

13. ILO, "Fundamental ILO Conventions," http://www.ilo.org/public/english/standards/norm/whatare/fundam/index.htm.

14. International Confederation of Free Trade Unions, "Internationally Recognized Core Labor Standards in the United States, Report for the WTO General Council Review of the Trade Policies of the United States," Geneva, July 1999.

15. Ibid., 2.

16. Ibid., 3.

17. As quoted in Philip S. Foner, *May Day: A Short History of the International Workers' Holiday, 1886–1986* (New York: International Publishers, 1986), 8.

18. Ibid., 12.

19. Ibid.

20. Ibid., 44–45.

21. It is exciting to see the rebirth of May Day organizing, first thanks to immigrant workers and more recently Occupy movement activists, and the growing participation of unions and their members.

22. Much useful information on the living-wage movement can be found in Robert Pollin and Stephanie Luce, *The Living Wage: Building a Fair Economy* (New York: New Press, 1998); and David Reynolds, "The Living Wage Movement Sweeps the Nation," *WorkingUSA*, September–October 1999.

23. Tragically, labor support groups are still fighting the same battles at these and other transnational corporations. The spotlight has recently been turned on the Chinese operations of Apple's primary subcontractor, Foxconn. See the website *China Labor Watch*, http://www.chinalaborwatch.org/.

24. For a critique of the FLA, see Medea Benjamin, "What's Fair about the Fair Labor Association? Putting the Fox in Charge," *Against the Current*, March–April 1999.

25. For discussion of the political significance of the anti-sweatshop movement, see Norm Diamond, "Anti-Sweat Politics," *Science as Culture* 8/4 (1999).

26. Daniel Singer, *Whose Millennium? Theirs or Ours?* (New York: Monthly Review Press, 1999), 230.

5. Learning from ALBA and the Bank of the South

This chapter is a revised and updated version of Martin Hart-Landsberg, "Learning from ALBA and the Bank of the South: Challenges and Possibilities," Monthly Review 61/4 (September 2009), which was also published in revised form (in Portuguese) as "ALBA and the Bank of the South," in Multilateralism and South American Reactions, *ed. Monica Dias Martins and Rosemary Galli (Ceara, Brazil: State University of Ceara Press, 2011).*

1. In 2009, the member countries of the Bolivarian Alternative for the Americas changed the name of the organization to the Bolivarian Alliance for the Americas.

2. Walden Bello, *Deglobalization: Ideas for a New World Economy* (New York: Zed Press, 2005), 43.

3. United Nations Conference on Trade and Development, *Trade and Development Report 1999* (New York: United Nations, 1999), chap. 4.

4. Mark Weisbrot, Dean Baker, and David Rosnick, "Scorecard on Development, 25 Years of Diminished Progress," Center for Economic Policy Research, September 2005, http://www.cepr.net/documents/publications/development_2005_09.pdf, 1.

5. See, for example, Kevin P. Gallagher and Lyuba Zarsky, *The Enclave Economy, Foreign Investment and Sustainable Development in Mexico's Silicon Valley* (Cambridge, MA: MIT Press, 2007); Enrique Dussel Peters, *Economic Opportunities and Challenges Posed by China for Mexico and Central America* (Bonn: German Development Institute, 2005).

6. Martin Hart-Landsberg and Paul Burkett, "China, Capital Accumulation, and Labor," *Monthly Review* 59/1 (May 2007).

7. Leandro Morais, "The 9th World Social Forum: New Pathways and Opportunities for the Global Alter-World Project," *CADTM*, February 27, 2009, http://cadtm.org/The-9th-World-Social-Forum-new.

8. In February 2012, at the 11th ALBA summit, St. Lucia and Suriname were granted special guest membership, with full membership awaiting only formal approval by their respective legislatures. Haiti was granted permanent observer status.

9. Chris Carlson, "First Meeting of ALBA Ministers Concludes in Venezuela," *Venezuelanalysis.com*, June 8, 2007, http://venezuelanalysis.com/news/2434.

10. In February 2012, at the 11th ALBA summit, the member countries agreed to contribute 1 percent of their international reserves to the ALBA Bank. See Rachel Boothroyd, "ALBA Advances toward 'Alternative Economic

Model,'" *The Bullet* 597 (February 13, 2012), http://www.socialistproject. ca/bullet/597.php.

11. Alejandro Bendana, "From Development Assistance to Development Solidarity: The Role of Venezuela and ALBA," International Development Economic Associates, February 14, 2008, http://www.networkideas.org/ alt/feb2008/alt14_Venezuela_ALBA.htm.

12. Shawn Hattingh, "ALBA: Creating a Regional Alternative to Neoliberalism?" *Venezuelananalysis.com*, February 13, 2008, http://venezuelanalysis.com/ analysis/3154

13. David Harris and Diego Azzi, *ALBA—Venezuela's Answer to "Free Trade"*: *The Bolivarian Alternative for the Americas*, Occasional Paper 3, Focus on the Global South, Bangkok, October 2006.

14. James Suggett, "ALBA Trade Bloc Forms Joint Food Company at Summit in Venezuela," *Venezuelanalysis.com*, February 3, 2009, http://venezuelanaly-sis.com/news/4165.

15. Kiraz Janicke, "Summit of the Bolivarian Alternative (ALBA) Concludes in Venezuela," *Venezuelanalysis.com*, January 27, 2008, http://venezuelanaly-sis.com/news/3104.

16. ALBA is also working to create new regional institutions. For example, an ALBA working group is developing plans for a regional arbitration center to handle disputes with foreign investors; several ALBA countries have already withdrawn from the World Bank–sponsored International Center for Settlement of Investment Disputes. ALBA nations are also considering the establishment of an ALBA commission on human rights to investigate charges of human rights violations as well as foreign-funded attempts to destabilize member countries.

17. Harris and Azzi, *ALBA—Venezuela's Answer to "Free Trade."*

18. "Sucre" comes from the Spanish initials for Sistem Unico de Compensacion Regional, or Unified System for Regional Compensation. The name was also chosen to honor Antonio Jose de Sucre, a Latin American indepen-dence fighter who fought with Simón Bolívar. This initiative is covered further in the next chapter.

19. The Sucre has an exchange value of $1.25.

20. Companies from Bolivia, Cuba, Ecuador, and Venezuela are currently trad-ing goods priced in Sucres. In the first half of 2011, a total of 77 companies from these countries engaged in Sucre-denominated trade worth $144 mil-lion. The relevant totals for the second half of 2010 were six companies and $40 million. Products traded include palm oil, textiles, medicine, veterinary products, tires, books, rice, powdered milk, and automobiles. See Correo del Orinoco International, "ALBA's Currency Grows," *Venezuelanalysis. com*, August 19, 2011, http://venezuelanalysis.com/news/6435.

21. This is especially true with the March 5, 2013, death of Venezuela's President Hugo Chávez.

22. Jodie Neary, "Venezuela's ALBA in the Face of the Global Economic Crisis," *UpsideDownWorld*, January 5, 2009, http://upsidedownworld.org/main/

venezuela-archives-35/1642-venezuelas-alba-in-the-face-of-the-global-economic-crisis-.

23. Gabriel Strautman, "South Bank: 90 Days of Silence," *CADTM*, April 2, 2008, http://cadtm.org/South-Bank-90-days-of-silence.

24. Oscar Ugarteche, "South American Countries Sign Banco del Sur Agreement," European Network on Debt and Development, *Eurodad.org*, October 19. 2009, http://eurodad.org/3882/. As of May 2012, only four of the seven countries—Venezuela, Ecuador, Bolivia, and Argentina—have given formal legislative approval to the bank's charter. Brazil, Paraguay and Uruguay have yet to take action.

25. Strautman, "South Bank."

26. Gabriel Elizondo, "Brazil's Powerhouse Bank," *Inter Press Service*, December 2, 2009. www.ipsnews.net/2009/12/develop-ment-brazils-powerhouse-bank/.

27. Eric Toussaint, "A Future for the Bank of the South?" *CADTM*, September 12, 2008, http://cadtm.org/A-Future-for-the-Bank-of-the-South.

28. Jubilee South et al., "Bank of the South: Second Open Letter to the Presidents of Argentina, Bolivia, Brazil, Ecuador, Paraguay, Uruguay and Venezuela," *CADTM*, December 7, 2007, http://cadtm.org/Second-open-letter-to-the.

29. Harris and Azzi, *ALBA—Venezuela's Answer to "Free Trade."*

30. Neary, "Venezuela's ALBA in the Face of the Global Economic Crisis."

31. This point has special meaning for East Asia, where many social movements are now trying to establish the kind of cross-border regional solidarity that exists in South America.

6. ALBA and the Promise of Cooperative Development

This chapter is a revised and updated version of Martin Hart-Landsberg, "ALBA and the Promise of Cooperative Development," Monthly Review 62/7 (December 2010).

1. Venezuela and Cuba signed the first ALBA exchange agreement in 2004. Bolivia joined in 2006, Nicaragua in 2007, Dominica and Honduras in 2008, and Ecuador, St. Vincent and the Grenadines, and Antigua and Barbuda in 2009. A U.S.-supported coup in Honduras installed a right-wing government that withdrew the country from ALBA in 2010. In February 2012, at the 11th ALBA summit, St. Lucia and Suriname were granted special guest membership, with full membership awaiting only formal approval by their respective legislatures. Haiti was granted permanent observer status. In 2009 the member countries of the Bolivarian Alternative for the Americas changed the name of the organization to the Bolivarian Alliance for the Americas.

2. Louis Bilbao, "Two Paths in the Face of Capitalism's Global Fracture," trans. Federico Fuentes, *LINKS, International Journal of Socialist Renewal*, 2009, http://links.org.au/node/817.

3. The Sucre's name comes from the Spanish initials for Sistem Unico de Compensacion Regional, or Unified System for Regional Compensation.

4. In February 2012, at the 11th ALBA summit, the eight ALBA members moved to formalize their efforts to create an integrated trade and financial zone by establishing a new economic integration plan to be called ECOALBA. ECOALBA is to encompass the ALBA Bank, Sucre finance system, and People's Trade Agreement. Its articles of agreement state that the aim of the initiative is to create "a shared-development, inter-dependent, sovereign and supportive economic zone aimed at consolidating and enlarging a new alternative model of economic relations that will strengthen and diversify the production apparatus and trade exchanges, as well as establishing the bases for the bilateral and multilateral instruments that the Parties may enter into on this matter, with a view to satisfying the physical and spiritual needs of our peoples." The agreement sets out general principles for "the planning and streamlining of economic relations among the Parties, by optimizing complementary productive and commercial linkages." See "Agreement for the Creation of the Economic Space of ALBA-TCP (ECOALBA-TCP)," www.alba-tcp.org/en/contenido/agreement-creation-economic-space-alba-tcp-ecoalba-tcp.

5. EPU membership included Austria, Belgium, Denmark, France, Germany, Greece, Iceland, Ireland, Italy, Luxembourg, the Netherlands, Norway, Portugal, Sweden, Switzerland, Trieste, Turkey, and the United Kingdom, as well as all countries and territories that were part of an existing European currency area.

6. William Diebold, *Trade and Payments in Western Europe: A Study in Economic Cooperation, 1947–51* (New York: Council on Foreign Relations/Harper, 1952), 217.

7. Ibid., 19–20; Fred L. Block, *The Origins of International Economic Disorder: A Study of United States International Monetary Policy from World War II to the Present* (Berkeley and Los Angeles: University of California Press, 1977), 237.

8. A few governments actually became reluctant to support further liberalization efforts, arguing that they would intensify already serious economic imbalances and employment problems. In response, some government officials sought to promote a planned (rather than market-driven) process of regional integration. Ultimately, OEEC governments rejected these proposals, in large part because European elites feared that they would strengthen new forms of public regulation and encourage a more politicized process for determining resource use. See Martin Hart-Landsberg, "ALBA and Cooperative Development: Lessons from the European Payments Union," *Marxism 21* 7/3 (2010): 400–403.

9. Jacob J. Kaplan and Guenther Schleiminger, *The European Payments Union, Financial Diplomacy in the 1950s* (Oxford: Clarendon Press, 1989), 31.

10. An ecu was set equal in value to the gold content of one U.S. dollar. This exchange relationship allowed the BIS to create a set of exchange rates between each European currency and the ecu.

11. The U.S. government successfully defeated this proposal. U.S. elites opposed it because it threatened the status of the U.S. dollar as the leading

international currency and would have forced the United States, as a leading surplus country, into significant policy changes.

12. In line with this history, the eleven European Union nations that created the euro area in 1999 also refused to introduce mechanisms requiring surplus as well as deficit nations to adjust their policies in response to regional trade imbalances. The heavy and growing adjustment costs generated by Germany's export offensive may well force one or more member countries to abandon the euro, leading to the eventual unraveling of the entire monetary union. See G. E. Krimpas, *The Recycling Problem in a Currency Union*, Working Paper No. 595, Levy Economics Institute (May 2010), http://www.levyinstitute.org/pubs/wp_595a.pdf.

13. Diebold, *Trade and Payments in Western Europe*, 123.

14. Kaplan and Schleiminger, *The European Payments Union*, 346.

15. Randal Hinshaw, "Toward European Convertibility," *Essays in International Finance* no. 31, International Finance Section, Department of Economics and Sociology, Princeton University, November 1958, 17.

16. At this time, there was little support within Europe for reductions in tariffs. The reason was that as members of the General Agreement on Trade and Tariffs European countries could not discriminate in their use of tariffs. In other words, if they offered tariff reductions to other OEEC countries, they would have been forced to extend the same reductions to countries outside the region.

17. Hinshaw, "Toward European Convertibility," 16.

18. Ibid., 17.

19. NAFTA is the North American Free Trade Agreement. AFTA is the ASEAN Free Trade Area. Mercosur is a South American free trade agreement. Neoliberal integration does not require a formal structure for its operations. For example, transnational corporations have created a China-centered, East Asian regional production system.

20. Companies from Bolivia, Cuba, Ecuador, and Venezuela are currently trading goods priced in Sucres. In the first half of 2011, a total of 77 companies from these countries engaged in Sucre-denominated trade worth $144 million. The relevant totals for the second half of 2010 were six companies and $40 million. Products traded include palm oil, textiles, medicine, veterinary products, tires, books, rice, powdered milk, and automobiles. See Correo del Orinoco International, "ALBA's Currency Grows," *Venezuelanalysis.com*, August 19, 2011, http://venezuelanalysis.com/news/6435.

21. ALBA governments have already announced their intention to create a supranational food enterprise, ALBA Alimentos, with the aim of boosting regional technological cooperation and training, rural infrastructure investment, and integrated food distribution.

22. For more on developments in Venezuela see Iain Bruce, *The Real Venezuela: Making Socialism in the 21st Century* (New York: Pluto Press, 2009); and Michael A. Lebowitz, *The Socialist Alternative: Real Human Development* (New York: Monthly Review Press, 2010).

Index